NUKED
A G.I. Memoir

Bob Ellis

Copyright © 2011 by Bob Ellis
All rights reserved, including the
right of reproduction in whole
or in part, in any form.

ISBN 978-1-937146-06-1

Printed and published by
Levellers Press
Amherst, Massachusetts

For all the hibakushi

CONTENTS

I
Leaving Home – 1
II
Basic – 5
III
In the Mud – 13
IV
Games – 21
V
Nostalgia – 29
VI
A Way Out – 37
VII
Sandia – 43
VIII
Special Weapons – 55
IX
Spies – 67
X
ORI – 79
XI
Kill – 92
XII
Killing Time – 101

XIII
The Brink – 111
XIV
Abandoned – 123
XV
Aftermath – 133
XVI
Deer Hunting – 137
XVII
Landslide – 147
XVIII
WSPG – 152
XIX
Playtime – 161
XX
The Pressure Is On – 171
XXI
Waffling – 181
XXII
Fat into the Fire – 191
XXIII
Airdrop – 201
XXIV
The End Game – 221

I
Leaving Home

On a Sunday, having long since taken to skipping Mass, I took a notion to drive down to Ed's place in the country, just to visit. The gas tank was full, and thinking I remembered the intricate route, was soon tracing the network of winding, hilly dirt roads, feeling good, enjoying my newfound mobility. The final leg of the way had changed, the road widened, banks lain back, curves gentled, grades evened out: no more chuck holes. I responded with a heavier foot, failing to notice that the road surface was thick with tiny pebbles, and when I started into a rising left-hand curve I noted with pleasure how competently the ungainly Dodge accelerated into the increasing steepness and curvature. No telling where my mind was when I overtook a battered yellow school bus tottering up the hill, full of black children. I was smart enough not to try to pass it on the left at risk of meeting oncoming traffic, but knew instantly the brakes wouldn't keep me from rear-ending the bus. Many calculations swirled through a mind made crackling sharp by kids' staring eyes in the back window. Everything went slow motion. The bus was rushing at me instead of the other way. My only remaining option was to swerve hard right, and immediately felt the ball-bearing road steal control. The old Dodge assertively zoomed into the drainage swale, climbed far up the naked bank before stopping, and then, as if grateful for a kinder fate, slowly rolled onto its side, top then other side, and came to rest in the swale with my door up.

Remembering to switch off the ignition, I opened the door and climbed out as from a hatch and jumped to the ground, breathing hard and shaking like it was ten below zero. I leaned against the car. When I had quit trembling a little, I lit a cigaret. At that moment a pickup appeared around the bend and the good ole boy driving it yelled out,

Git away from that gas tank! – I jumped away instantly, cursing myself. The guy stopped. He was not unsympathetic and in a jerky conversation with him I got a message to Ed whom he knew, and when Ed appeared I had regained my idiotic bravado and announced a decision just made:

Nothing left to do now but join the Army...

I hadn't even made the first payment on the damned car.

I sold its remains for a song to Bobby Harkness, and a few mornings later travelled by bus to Alexandria and talked with a sergeant in the store-front recruiting station facing the Masonic Temple. Shortly after that I had got my ducks in a row and told my parents what I planned to do, to their shocked surprise. Of the morning when the Army was to send a vehicle to bring me to Alexandria for induction, there remains a memory, a tableau in which my inner spectator, at full alert, let me stand beside myself: I am standing facing them at the extremity of the wide green lawn in bright May sunshine, birds singing, trees leafing out, suddenly seeing my Mom and Dad as old people – at 42 and 44 respectively. Taking leave was awkward; clumsy bravado shielded my nervousness. Suddenly I was motor-mouthing, chattering about college and the G.I. Bill of Rights for which I would be eligible afterward. At a certain point, minutes dwindling away – the sergeant had said the driver would be punctual – my mother asked me to "be careful," and I retorted cheerfully,

Don't worry, Mom, I won't make a Gold Star mother of you – meaning the window decal the War Department "awarded" to families who had "lost" a son or a father – but few daughters – to war. She answered me immediately, completely astonishing me:

You're damn right you won't!

I was speechless at her emotion, struck by the pain behind her words, and saw all at once that they were both actually if not tearfully upset. I asked her,

What do you mean by that? I saw tears as she said roughly, a catch in her throat, almost savagely,

I'd never let them put one of those things in my window,

Instantly I wanted to hear more from this woman I had never in my life heard express a political view, and later realized that was the only swear word I ever heard her utter. (She died at advanced age having never exercised her franchise as a free American.) But it was too late: just then the stubby olive-drab bus pulled up. I shook my dad's hand, tried unsuccessfully to hug my mom and then it was off to the induction center where I was weighed, measured, bled, tested for literacy, poked, prodded, questioned and after some hours found myself in the front room again, standing alongside half a dozen other boys in front of the sergeant, who prepared to administer the oath of allegiance to us.

Repeat after me, said the sergeant and we all did, line by line, but at the end I deliberately kept my mouth shut when everybody else said "So help me God." Hardly a half a day from home I was determined to start thinking and acting like the atheist I believed I was. The sergeant told us to take one step forward. One goofus made the sign of the cross. The sergeant smirked grimly and said,

Thass right, boys, you might as well give your heart and soul to Jee-zus, cuz I got yer ass.

II
Basic

Shortly we were on an Army bus bound for Fort George George Meade over in Maryland, that was its actual name then, no bullshit, I thought it was a howler. Anybody whose parents had branded him like that must have been really screwed up and the Army was the right place for him.

The violence began immediately. Just one surreal scene of subhuman drear will tell it, maybe on the first afternoon. Scared and sheepish, we were assigned to KP ("kitchen police") in a vast yellow-walled dining hall. From the start I acted as if my every move would be dictated, including release from whatever duty. Unbelievable it seems now. For hours on end I cleaned and re-cleaned kitchen equipment, mopped acres of red-tiled floors, scrubbed spotless latrines – for 34 hours nonstop. The end came in the wee hours. We were standing in place, like wind-up toys with springs run down, leaning chin-on-hands atop our mop handles, some of us dozing. Along came a corporal-cook who, passing one of us perched zombies, casually but deliberately kicked his mop from under, dumping the unfortunate boy, who gashed his chin and broke some teeth. Immediately there was protest. Groggy and stupified, I didn't start it. Witnesses jangled awake at the bored viciousness of the deed, noisy, like engines starting cold. The protest rose and echoed as nearby guys hurried to the injured man; somebody hollered about complaining to the Mess Sergeant and went off to find him. It seemed to re-awaken me to a kind of unthinking wildness: I was no slave, enough of this shit. Without waiting to hear about justice done or not done, I left in the dark for my bunk, filled with anxiety, fearing I might be going AWOL...

Newly uniformed and dogtagged, we were crowded onto a pokey troop train that wound for sixteen hours up the Potomac river, then south through the mountains of West Virginia, headed for Camp Breckenridge ("Brokenback"), where our new First Sergeant barked us into proper formation, looked us over and told us acidly we were "a sorry lot, no doubt about it" – but, he said, we were no longer boys, but *men*.

And if you aren't, or don't want to be, you let me know right now and we'll take care of you...and as far as you're concerned, my word is law, and if you think that's tough, you're right; I was where you are once; I took it and I'm still here, and now it's my turn. He smiled evilly, let his words sink in.

Now we'll get along al-right, if you remember a few things, which you will learn more about di-rectly.

Now, I'm no officer, and I cain't make you do a damn thing. But I can sure as hell make you wish you had, and you'd better believe that. Lastly, I don't want to hear no SIR from you men; and if you got all that, I wanna hear you say YES, SERGEANT!

Lamely we answered, not nearly loudly enough, had to do it again and keep doing it until the suddenly deaf sergeant finally heard us.

In due course we were assigned to a company in a battalion in a regiment of the famous 101st Airborne Division, distributed into platoons and squads, shorn of hair and issued everything we needed to start fighting the next day. My rifle was an M-1 Garand, a gas-operated autoloader, .30 caliber, heavy and old and use-worn. I had to treat it as if it were brand new, keep it immaculate and ready for inspection at any time. Performing before us, the sergeant warned us not to call it a 'gun.' Shaking the weapon and grabbing his crotch with his other hand, he roared at us,

THIS IS MY RIFLE, THIS IS MY GUN; THIS IS FOR BUSINESS, THIS IS FOR FUN... Lemme HEAR you... Anybody who forgets and calls that rifle a GUN is gonna SLEEP with it!

Thus we sank into the morass, hounded by loud-mouthed bad-tempered non-coms, into the stumbling puppetry of close-order drill and the Manual of Arms, endless marching, inspections at rigid attention, mired in shameful subservience, numb with fatigue like nothing I'd ever known: stripped buck-naked and dehumanized, calculatedly and precisely – like millions of men have endured to look back on – if they survived – with a warm holy nostalgia hardly distinguishable from reverence.

First barracks inspection: pure terror. After chow, toilets spotless, floors scrubbed white, butt-cans emptied and re-sanded, we stood at the foot of our bunks without rifles, footlockers open.

Tench-HUT! – the sergeant marched imperiously through the double doors flanked by grim-faced corporals. Surveying the room, he explained that when he gave the order, we were to be "at ease." When he approached somebody, that man would snap to, salute and announce his name rank, and serial number, and too bad if he hadn't memorized it yet. This would be the one and only time we'd ever salute a non-commissioned officer; his job was to teach us how to treat real officers. "At ease" meant stand feet apart, hands behind backs, immobile.

If you got that, I want to hear you say, "YES SERGEANT!"
YES SERGEANT!
Cain't hear ya!
YES SERGEANT!
Better - still WEAK!
YES SERGEANT!
At ease!

The sergeant's first victim was Hickey from Pittsburgh. He stood there looking that boy up and down, a sneer on his face, but found nothing to say. Then he turned his attention to Hickey's footlocker; he spied something crimson partly visible beneath the top drawer.

What's this? he said, pulling out a garish velveteen cushion, highly scented with cheap perfume. He held it up with two fingers for all to see.

I ast you – WHAT IS THIS? That boy's face was as red as the dangled pillow. He mumbled something. Somebody snickered.

WHAT GIRL FRIEND? shouted the sergeant, *You ain't GOT no girl friend; this is Camp Breckenridge, Kaintucky; this is Basic Training, the ARMY, and I don't wanna hear no more about no girl friend. And I don't want to see this...this THANG ...ever again; you got it?*

Yes, sir.
WHAD YOU CALL ME?
YES SERGEANT.

The sergeant suddenly turned to the man next to Hickey.

And you – what're YOU laughing at? That one was totally discombobulated; he had understood how the inspection would unfold, and here was this angry sergeant addressing him without giving him the chance to come to attention, salute and give his name, rank and serial number. After a short pause, the sergeant tense before him, he mumbled,

Nothing... Now the sergeant was in his face; like Hickey he turned red, went into "attention," head up like a bittern hiding, staring straight ahead.

WHAT'S SO FUNNY? The man mumbled nearly inaudibly, something about "souvenirs from home."

And what about you? You got any "souvenirs" from home? You got a girl friend back home too?

No, I don't. I've only got my Bible.

No girl friend, eh? What's the matter with you? You look like a man... The snickerer was now redder than Hickey had been. I thought I could see trembling. But the sergeant wasn't through with him yet.

No girl, eh... What's the matter with you? he said, putting his face inches from his victim's... *You got tendencies, boy? You got no girl friend, you laugh at him for havin one... I think you got tendencies, what do you say to that? SPEAK UP!*

That was my first witness of breakdown under stress. This sarcastic meanness was more than a good Christian draftee could take. The poor guy was weeping, sobbing, blubbering about being God-fearing and only wanting to get this over with and go back where he came from. Immediately, without changing his tone of voice, the sergeant backed off.

Well, let me tell you, private, I ain't exactly here cuz I wanna be either. But I got a job to do, and you got a job to do, and we'll just have to make the best of it, and I want you to start acting like a man. At ease, private!

Thus it went, down the long room, slowly and methodically, stiff hard-eyed non-coms delving into open footlockers, barren receptacles symbolic of us new non-persons. The sergeant carefully avoided personal photos, crucifixes, mezzuzas and the like. There was more: specimens of the insipid pornography of those dreary years. Whether the sergeant confiscated the dismal stuff is lost. The owner of a paperback copy of *God's Little Acre* was allowed to keep it after mildly defending it, which provoked the sergeant into a long speech about why we were all there, but which did not include mention of the Bill of Rights. Waiting, I wondered if they'd uncover my high school ring, the only thing connecting me to my past except for the old Boy Scout knife in my pocket. When they stopped in front of me, I saluted stiffly, feeling foolish at my nervous exaggeration of the ritual, sounded off, name rank and serial number...

RA, huh? He looked me up and down. *So – you gonna be a professional, private?*

I don't know, sergeant. Maybe. He continued to examine me, then said,

Well, if you got...aspirations, private, you start by standing closer to your razor tomorrow morning. Till that moment, I had thought I didn't have enough hair on my face to shave every day.

Yes, sergeant. It finished long after lights-out. The guys ribbed me loudly about being a "professional." Defensive, my reaction was to explain myself:

I'm here mainly to get the G.I Bill.

A draftee from Philadelphia said,

Hell of a way to get ahead in the world – join the fuckin' army in wartime!

Early on we got our first lesson in military justice. A black man, a draftee from Chicago, balked at some order. The sergeant called an officer, who repeated the command three times to make sure the man understood, who refused each time. We were all summoned to ranks then. The lieutenant spoke slowly and clearly, making sure we all heard. He told the obdurate private he had one more chance. If he refused the order again, it would be "company punishment" or "court martial," his choice. Did he understand? The man nodded. Was he now ready to obey the order?

No.

An additional offense, refusing to address an officer as "sir;" he merely shrugged when asked his choice of punishment; the lieutenant made the decision.

Company punishment meant sending for The Major, an ill-mannered martinet who announced his displeasure at having to deal with such petty crap while Real Men were dying in Korea.

He recited the facts of the matter, proclaimed the charge, insubordination, and gave the rebel a chance to respond. The man remained mute. The major then set the punishment: to dig a hole beside the barracks six by six feet, six feet deep. A supply corporal provided a shovel and showed him the location. The conscript, seemingly humbled, set to work in the hot sun and gradually dug himself out of sight, finishing just before Mess Call. The Major was summoned again; stiffly he examined the hole, made a show of measuring it though he had nothing to measure with – then walked up face-to-face to the sweat-stained private, told him it was "good work"; then he paused, looked into the man's eyes and said softly,

Now, soldier, fill it back up!

At this the private's eyes opened wide and white as the words sunk in; for a few seconds he stared at the major, his shiny black face expressing what I would have called *dementia*; he relaxed into profound and doleful lassitude, then opened his hand almost casually and let the shovel drop clattering into the hole. Those nearest heard him mumble,

If you want that mothafucka filled up, you kin fill it yo'self.

SERGEANT! yelled the Major, *arrest that man and take him to the brig!*

Yes SIR!

How the hole was refilled I never heard. Thornberry from Tennessee, the only other black man in the company, was a cheerful, copper-skinned basketball player, whom I thought had some training as a preacher. We asked him what he thought of this situation and he said,

These Chicago boys can be tough cases, yessir, I mean tough cases, hear-me-what-I-say, what-I-say cuz I hardly ever says it, that boy was tough!

But he wouldn't say anything more, and I understood his caginess; he knew exactly where he was, candor would be stupidity. Marching double time as usual a day or so later, we saw the hapless Chicago guy wearing leg irons and striped fatigues, walking down the road in front of an MP with a sawed-off shotgun.

A couple weeks into training I was summoned to the post dentist who, examining my mouth with an expression of increasing sadness, told me what was coming, then performed vigorous and unspeakable acts on my upper and lower jaws. After the surgery, mouth stuffed with cotton, stuck in the butt with a painful B-vitamin shot, I left in sweltering heat to trek back to the company. Sweat-soaked and dizzy when I got to the barracks, I found my bunk and lay down. Some corporal woke me after a while, told me to report for duty with the company. Inarticulate from the massive novocaine, I told him I'd lost a lot of blood and was sick; I needed to rest. This was my first ever brush with real trauma, entangled as it was with the life I'd fled – all those kids, no money for dentistry – and of course I had never in my life given a thought to anything 'preventive'…

The corporal threatened disciplinary action, but I was floating in a void where nothing whatsoever mattered. I told him to do what he had to do, that I'd be here when he was ready for me…

III
In the Mud

Basic training reduced us to behavioral plasticity. Under a wrathful cadre, the company gradually warped itself into numb coherence as a unit. United by common hardship we diffidently began to relate to one another, find out who we were in chit-chat between times, bitching in chow lines or polishing boots and brass before lights out. I couldn't have cared less about the chatter of my barracks-mates, nothing but cars and women and beer. With no privacy, Mail Call our only luxury, which might bring a *CARE* package from home, personal treasures quickly secreted in footlockers and consumed mostly in the dark, we were always scrutinizing each other, effectively policing behavior, our own and others, occasionally to loud argument. All officers were to be hated on principle; sergeants were no better. With corporals you were on your own, you hoped he wasn't bucking for stripes.

One Friday night that sarcastic draftee from Philadelphia loudly demanded our attention. It took him a while to break through boisterous evening gabble, even after resorting to strong language. Finally he stood atop his footlocker and reported that his "shaving bomb" was missing and demanded to know who took it. He got no response beyond vocal sympathy, and after pleading and cajolling, asserting that he didn't mind the "borrowing," he knew how it was, we were all equal, making $99 a month and he might have to borrow something himself some time, so that was OK, but he needed it to shave for inspection in the morning. He waited. The aerosol didn't turn up. Looking disappointed, his voice dropping in pitch, he spoke in rich stentorian tones,

Alright, if that's the way it's gonna be, if we can't live together without stealing from each other, then that's too bad, we'll all put padlocks on our footlockers, but we'll get through this, we won't be together forever...

His words trailed off, but he continued with narrowed eyes – *and by the way, whoever stole my shaving cream, HIS MOTHER AND FATHER SLEEP IN SHIT!*

At this, unbelievably, a guy a few bunks down responded to the statement, angrily; the theft victim, known henceforth as a "Philadelphia lawyer," advanced on the angry one, who stopped his outburst in midstream and shut his mouth, but too late. Philadelphia proceeded to subject him to sly interrogation, face-to-face cross-examination about the nature of his anger. The man hemmed and hawed defensively and finally said he was only objecting to the bad language, nothing else. The guys now circling round hooted at him. Philadelphia continued to press him patiently, gently but relentlessly, and in the end manipulated the man into opening his footlocker, revealing the missing shaving cream... We gasped.

Just then, copper-skinned Thornberry broke out in loud laughter, began to orate in "preacher" mode, developing an amazing performance of incantation and singsong and holy-roller armwaving, largely unintelligible for some minutes until we began to see he was slyly giving us a message: Don't persecute this thief, this poor boy was just like the rest of us, had made a mistake like any of us could, maybe had, *probably* had, only he got caught and was full of shame now, he'd been punished enough already and probably learned his lesson – and at the same time Preacher was praising Philadelphia's lawyerly performance, saying he really got it, he did things right, this could have been real bad but it wasn't; and winding down he made precise, accurate jabs at everybody in the room, not once mentioning religion or names, and soon had us all laughing, even the culprit, and then some guys began to praise *his* performance, but he waved it all off as if it didn't mean a thing and went on laughing until we went back to our own stuff, to the showers or boot-polishing...That was for me a valuable but long-latent lesson in conflict resolution, for Thornberry's performance really did smooth it over, made things right again, without anything nasty.

That may have been the same night we returned to barracks late after a live-fire exercise in which we learned we could actually shoot effectively by starshine. That might come in handy, we were told. The Chinese coming into Korea liked to carry out screaming night-time assaults. Saturday inspection the next morning held greater stakes than usual: a hint of a weekend pass if the inspection went with no "demerits." Dog-tired from yesterday's march, I turned in without cleaning my rifle. An early riser, I counted on doing it before inspection, but woke up after others were moving around. I was late! Boots not polished, no time to clean the bore of the damned rifle, let alone its gas piston. I took a chance that the lieutenant, who frequently didn't look down barrels, would pass me up this time. I misjudged. Expecting the same lieutenant as usual, I was shocked when another man walked through the door. The sergeant hollered "Tench-hut!" Sinking feelings as we jumped to. The inspection was thorough and slow. I was only slightly comforted by other guys getting demerits – the blame would not be mine alone if we didn't get passes. The sergeant was writing everything down.

Second Lieutenant Green was Alabaman, a soft-spoken, easy-going, newly minted infantry officer probably bound for Korea like us. He wanted to know where I was from. Tense, not ready, I said,

Virginia. I'd been asked this question many times by now, but it still rankled – I don't know why – what a stupid notion, being "from" someplace or other...

Oh, another Rebel, eh? Virginia a good place to be from, private?

I didn't know how to take his question, thought there might be a trick in it, decided to play it straight,

Yes, sir. Green smiled at me. Unable to bend, fixated on my dirty M-1, I took refuge in military formalism with this smooth-faced and sandy-haired officer who for all I knew could bite like an alligator. Green looked me up and down a few seconds, then said in the same easy-going conversational tone,

Present arms.

I slammed the bolt open, snapped the rifle in front of me for him to take, which he did, informally again, continuing low-key chatter while he examined the piece. Shortly he angled the rifle to peer into the muzzle. His smile slowly faded. He handed the rifle back. I took it and waited for the order, but Green merely said,

Be at ease, and stood studying me. *You evah been on a train, Virginia?*

I nodded.

Been through a tunnel?

I nodded again.

Evah seen that little spot of light in the black, way off in the distance?

I nodded a third time, seeing what was coming; the sergeant was glaring at me, writing on his clipboard.

Yes, sir.

Well, Virginia, Ah've looked daown moah rifle barrels than Ah could evah count, and Ah don't, Ah really don't believe Ah've evah seen a dirtier one...

Yes, sir.

Naow, Ah know you-all were on the night-fire range las' night... He paused to study me, then said,

You know, wheah you-all ah goin', you will sholy find out that this piece could be the bes' friend you evah had. You don'

know that yet – maybe you won't ever – 'cause if you did, cleanin' that rifle woulda been the first thing you did when you got back heah las' night, draggin' ass or not...

Yes, sir...

Thass all, Virginia.

We got no weekend pass, nor would for weeks. When it was over acrimony broke out, apportioning and particularizing blame for the failure. I was meek and took no part, relieved to share the blame, glad I wasn't the only demerit goofball.

Bull, somebody said, *It's policy, no passes are ever given the first eight weeks of basic.* Somebody else said "Bull" to that. It didn't matter to me, I had no idea what I would do with a weekend pass. I had to admit Eberhard's wisdom. He had warned me to clean my rifle before sleep like everybody else.

Outside training, I made no friends, and seldom wondered why. Part of it was, I was "RA" – a Regular Army volunteer in an outfit of draftees. They could bitch about anything and everything, and did. I couldn't complain because I'd asked for this shit. They'd be out in two years, I was stuck for three. I'd seen possibility of friendship with Eberhard, but I didn't follow through. Eberhard, who may have had some college before being drafted, hated guns, wanted to be a medic. I was attracted to him at first for a casual nurturing quality he held out in an off-hand way to all and sundry, with no trace of religious do-gooder motivation. But he was openly implacable in opposition to guns, for any reason, including hunting. He was honest in a way I wasn't. I would have first had to believe that anyone could actually care for me, which I didn't, let alone it be a man.

The guys were vocal about getting off post, for beer, women and dancing. You couldn't get to Evansville and back on a weekend without a car, but you could make it to the county seat, where you could get real beer, not the horse-piss available on post, which had to be finagled illicitly in any case, beer being "Off Limits" to trainees. Even when we managed to bootleg some, it was only some weird, watery brew from Missouri or Kansas with a German name we immediately dubbed "Greasy Dick."

What did I do with free time when it came? The grumpy Army maxim was literally true: hurry up and wait. But life wasn't only polishing brass and boots. Chronic fatigue alternated with boredom in endless rounds: standing formation, marching, KP, pushups and PT. Off hours I slept. There was little to read, but we somehow learned of the execution of Julius and Ethel Rosenberg, which provoked loud discussion in the barracks, in which I took no part, feeling I had no understanding of what treason was, as if that *only* was what counted. I wrote few letters home, only when I got one, only after procrastination born of a sour brew I couldn't have named. My mind stayed away from the "past." The Army had stamped my dogtags with a "C" – for Christian or Catholic – despite my weak protest, but that recruiting sergeant wasn't about to leave the blank unfilled, noting that "St. Anthony's High School" was diagnosis enough.

Withstanding boredom, part self-incarceration, part unthinking obedience – came uncommonly easily to me. Others noticed my propensity to silence, hence left me alone. We were all too tired for the bedtime banter of earlier days. The abrasive routine of the unending weeks wafted away in perpetual low-grade discomfort somehow gotten through, hazy memories of heat and dust and boot polish, the brassy brilliance of the Kentucky sun, the barracks-stink of sweaty feet, of bodies worked hard, the acrid tang of after-shave, days punctuated by "Dear John" letters followed perhaps by muffled sobs that night, and yet another tour of KP where I kept my head down to avoid the wrath of the Mess Sergeant who would send you to clean out some loathsome grease trap if he didn't like your looks.

The rasping degradation applied equally to women – Breckenridge trained WACs too, the Women's Army Corps. On a march one morning "Hup-two-three-four" we passed a lecture hall. From within came a loud, plainly female voice at angry volume as we passed windows open to the heat:

When I give the command I wanna hear forty snappin' pussies hit those chairs with one sound, you got it? Now – MOVE! Apparently they didn't get it, despite loud thumps and bangs, for the unseen drill instructor put her charges through the process again as we passed by in general amusement, snickers and whoops – and sympathy from some – and got reprimanded by our own drill instructor, trying lamely to hide his own grin. The sexual segregation was complete: I never saw a woman on that post, not a WAC or even a nurse.

One day we marched out to bunkered pits, the hand grenade range. Gaffney said he didn't think he could handle throwing a live grenade. He was slender and short, left-handed and seemed of poor motor coördination. He was always getting yelled at for falling out of step – just a boy he was, almost childlike and likeable for that. We all encouraged him, told him it would be easy, showed him the motions. You walked well into the bunker, a three-sided earthen revetment, the inside walls lined with heavy logs. All you had to do was pull the pin and toss the damn thing over any wall. We'd practiced with duds, it was easy as pie, but Gaffney shook his head mournfully – he remembered that when the handle released on throwing, the grenade would explode just eight seconds later.

Time that with your watch, the sergeant said, *plenty of time.* Then he added, unconsciously lowering his voice, *grenades have been known to go off sooner, but almost never.*

Gaffney's turn came; he was shaking, saying he was no good at throwing, never could play ball. A cadre-man positioned himself behind Gaffney's right side, told him,

Just pull the pin and toss it over; you don't have to throw it far. You can do it. With much hesitation, Gaffney accepted the grenade, paused, then pulled the pin and flung the bomb as hard as he could: it went nearly straight up. The cadreman smacked him to the ground with the flat of his hand and flopped on top of him. Waiting our turn, we gasped and broke formation to run away. The grenade came down just outside the bunker and went off with the loudest detonation I'd ever heard. In a second or two it rained minute gritty shrapnel over us, now yards away and being yelled at to *Fall in!*

Gaffney apologized abjectly on his way back to ranks, saying he was sorry, but he "knew something was gonna happen." Cynics in the ranks intimated that he was just play-acting – "Just a goddam goldbrick," they said, trying to influence the Army with this phony incompetence not to send him into combat. In my gut I felt sympathy for him, appalled that they might put this poor bastard who didn't know his ass from page eight into combat.

Things changed after our eighth-week "graduation" inspection and parade. Coming up was "Heavy Weapons" training, eight more weeks of the same shit. Harassment, extreme fatigue, huge meals, yelled lectures, endless marching, random chickenshit inspections, every minute occupied from dawn till lights out. Running double-time everywhere, ten pull-ups before allowed into the mess hall, raw young bodies being toughened up for slaughter. I believed I saw through what they were doing to us: making sure we felt everything required to kill another human on sight. Bayonet practice, full-pack route marches to distant firing ranges, we learned to shoot everything they had that threw hot metal with a bang. Ever more often we were reminded that we were bound for a real shooting war.

IV
Games

We bivouacked in steamy, tick-infested woods, simulated combat; we reached the area after a five mile route march on dirt roads, fitted out in full field gear, canteens, packs, pup tents, steel helmets, rifles with bayonets, and told to dig foxholes. The first guys finished were grabbed to dig a slit trench latrine for the platoon. The sergeant told us to buddy up – two to a tent, he urged – told us we'd be playing the Green side in a war game against Reds who would probably come from *that* way, but might come from any direction. We had to "establish a perimeter" and mount guard duty, two-hour rotations starting at 2100 hours until dawn. Anyone caught sleeping on guard would be punished. He didn't say how. All this would only teach us "a little something, just a little" about what a shooting war was like, say Korea, where terrorizing night assaults were routine. But sometimes it seemed to me, trying to take this stuff seriously, that the cadre all held back, were less than candid about what we'd face "over there," and could have said much more.

What I'm here for is to show you everything I can to make sure you come back alive. There's no way I can make you bulletproof, I wish I could but I cain't. All I can do is to show you men some of the stupid ways you can catch a bullet and chew yer ass if I see you doin em. Now some of you might have heard another bullshit rumor last week about a truce over there. That's just a rumor, got it? Even if they call a cease-fire, don you believe it, you keep that rifle handy at all times!

We had dug in as ordered before dark. A rumor went round that some corporals were going to sneak away in a jeep after dark for beer. I was too tired to be interested, and spent the evening hanging around my pup tent and foxhole, smoking and watching for chiggers, which had already bitten some. Somewhere I found straw to put under my sleeping bag, meager protection against the bare stony ground. I had not found a buddy to hook up with; most guys had. The fact is, I didn't look for one, and couldn't have said why not. I opened some C-rations, ate them without bothering with "Sterno," cold, greasy pork sausage patties with zero spices. From my canteen I dripped water onto hardtack biscuits in their tin, watched them puff up and become soft enough to gum. By now I could eat corn on the cob, even steak. When it got dark I unrolled my sleeping bag and stretched out. It was quiet, but I was far from sleepy; this was my first ever "camping out." Dreamy, near exhaustion but restless when I wanted to sleep, I was fantasizing about the ultimate decision: to deliberately kill a human being...We'd heard the scuttlebutt of GIs bayonetted in their sleeping bags at Chosin Reservoir because they couldn't exit fast enough. Sleeping bags had been redesigned, it was said. New zippers let the occupant bust out quickly. The light wool bags issued for this exercise had old style zippers, but nobody needed to zip up on this hot dank night. I hadn't the foggiest notion whether I could ever pull the trigger on a man. My morbid pondering lost steam gradually, but not before I thought, or perhaps decided, that unless you made a positive, conscious choice to shoot, which made you a murderer, you just had to wait until the actual situation arose; probably I would shoot if a gun were pointed at me.

The war game was a farce of mysterious commands and senseless running around and hard-to-identify Red troops; we had unlimited blank ammo and basically we spent the day running from one patch of woods to another, firing off our rifles at nothing in particular. It made me think back to cap-pistol games with my brothers out in Bascom's pasture, realizing that was not so long ago! But things were different now – this was make-believe *but not* at the same time, unnerving.

During one "skirmish" I thought I could tell where some Reds were by gunfire, but couldn't see a soul until, through a screen of saplings, I made out the figure of a man, saw the flash of a gold bar, a second lieutenant. He was wearing a red armband, half-crouched, paying attention to something behind him. *His men*, I thought. I started to raise my rifle, but all at once was overcome, seized with emotional paralysis. These were only blanks, but I could not aim at the officer, who was unaware of me. I was baffled, frozen; but had to do something, so I lowered the M1 and fired from the hip BLAM! BLAM! BLAM! then ran away hard, not knowing why I did so, feeling somehow abnormal, crazy. Now, I know my response was perfectly sane, and by inversion I see that it is military culture that is insane, truly so.

Maneuvers went on another full day; dig foxholes in time to abandon them, run here and there and back again. At one point I hid out under a tree, to rest and smoke, early afternoon, the heat of the day. No one was around, no shooting nearby, and I dozed off, but awakened to a sensation like distant yet somehow serious heat in my midsection. I jumped up, threw off the web belt, my belly and right hip suddenly on fire. Then my right ankle caught the same fire, and in near panic I opened my pants, discovered welts, saw tiny red dots creeping around. Cursing, I brushed the chiggers to their death, moved into thicker brush and undressed all the way, took off boots, pants, underwear, searched out the tiny demons, repeatedly snapped my pants, rubbed their legs together thoroughly, thinking somebody would come along and catch me any minute, and dressed again. After a long time the fiery welts on my belly subsided to intense itching, far worse than any poison ivy endured back home. As if building a legal case, I counted 37 chigger-bites around my middle where the wide canteen belt had constricted my fatigues.

Later that afternoon, I went to the latrine in its grove; someone had cut two forked sapling stakes and jammed them into the ground at either end of the foul trench; a sitting-pole rested on the forks, and while making myself comfortable as possible to do what I'd come for, shooting suddenly started nearby and Lieutenant Green and some guys broke out of the brush running, everybody looking at my bare butt, Green hollering as he ran past,

Break it off in the middle, Virginia, we got work to do...
Uncomfortable, itching, constipated – no green vegetables or fruit for days – I was instantly resentful and tuned out the damned interruption – let the crazy bastards go! I wondered how often guys die in combat circumstances like this. My rifle was yards away, leaning against a sapling.

That night, exhausted again and lonely, I sought out the beer, stashed with ice in the Lister bag hanging beside the big field tent of the cadre. Through a screen I could see a sergeant I didn't know and other non-coms sitting at a table playing cards. I gave six bits for a beer to a corporal who came along and took my coins. He made a point of saying,

The money's not mine to keep, and don come back for another one.

In the sack, sore in every muscle, scheduled for guard duty in the last rota before dawn, I sucked up the beer, thinking about that lieutenant I couldn't fire at. I was not at all homesick, I had no home. I fell into some half-thought having to do with "intent to kill" and soon dozed off, a lit cigaret in my fingers. Nightmarishly I awakened to stinging smoke, saw small flames and realized what had happened. I pounded out the flames creeping across the straw toward my sleeping bag. I burned a wrist in the snuffing. Eberhard was nearby. He gave me burn ointment, but couldn't resist chastising me for smoking at all, let alone doing it in the sack. Later I realized I'd treated him churlishly in my chagrin. Eberhard wasn't obliged to treat me, he wasn't a real medic, and when I tried to apologize, he shrugged and said,

I'd rather you quit smoking than listen to apologies.

Later, shots somewhere in the night woke me, not far off. I saw muzzle flashes, heard hollering. We'd been told of possible infiltration by Reds during the night, and had been given passwords in case this happened. If we whispered the password and didn't hear the correct "countersign" we could shoot. Some of our own guys, more gung-ho than me for sure, were out similarly trying to infiltrate a Red perimeter if they could find one, and would be returning toward dawn, so the password system could have value. Coming fully awake, I saw a flashlight – only cadre had them – then heard angry talk coming my way. After a bit the light stopped moving and I heard Eberhard say,

Show me the place; roll up your pantleg.

And then,

Yes, I see it; it's probably going to be a bruise; but it's not a burn, and the skin isn't broken, so you're okay.

Then I heard the victim's voice; it was Philadelphia; he'd been shot in the leg, hit by wadding from the blank cartridge as he tried to re-enter the perimeter; he swore he'd given the correct countersign when challenged but was shot anyway. He was angry, full of ominous threats of what would happen when he found out who pulled that trigger. When it was over Eberhard passed by and I asked the *de facto* corpsman what time it was: 3:30 AM. No sense going back to sleep. I was due to relieve Campbell in a half hour. I dressed and sat in the black moist night smoking and drinking water, my blistered wrist sore, mouth foul and cottony. Faint red began to streak up the darkness and I went to my guard post, let Campbell go. *So that's east.* It grew quiet again and I had to concentrate to stay awake. I had no idea where in the world I was, tried to imagine this spot as if from a great height but couldn't, had no notion whatever about roads, creeks, towns, mountains, or *anything* natural. I didn't even know what kind of tree I'd been sleeping under…

Part of the applied psychology of basic, I figured, was calculated to keep us in the dark as much as possible, to approximate the chaos of real combat. Hence I was greatly and pleasantly surprised, going off guard duty as the brassy sun came up, to hear we were done, no more of this war-game crap, this organized grab-ass as Philadelphia called it. We would break camp and march back to post today. I itched miserably from chigger bites, had never smelt so foul to myself in my life, couldn't wait to get to a shower. After awhile the cadre rounded up the unspent blank ammo, told us to gather our shit together. There would be an "inventory inspection" on reaching barracks, to see what was missing – but don't worry, loss and breakage of equipment was expected in field exercises. When we assembled for the return march, I discovered I had no canteen. Its cup was still there in the canvas belt holder. We waited. It got hot, then hotter. The sun rose and still we waited, the rising heat eventually smothering our bitching. Under the trees the chiggers got you, out in the sun you roasted; screwed either way.

At length they gathered us up and we marched informally back to post. Before allowing us indoors, the sergeant tallied up equipment losses, making sarcastic references to "grown men" who hadn't learned how to hold onto stuff, especially canteens. Mine was the only item I couldn't account for. In a day or two, I was called to the supply room and questioned again. The sergeant had sarcastically witnessed my loss, yet these two hard-eyed supply corporals were openly skeptical of my statement that only my canteen was missing.

Are you sure? That's not what we heard.

What do you mean? I said.

Well there's this piece of paper you signed, saying you're missing a fartsack, a canteen and a mess kit.

I didn't sign any paper, I said, *I only lost a canteen.*

At that point one of them rummaged around a desk drawer and came up with some kind of official-looking Quartermaster form I'd never seen. At the bottom was my name in ink – but clearly not in my handwriting.

That's not my signature. An argument ensued. Suddenly I was embattled and stubborn. I had not signed a thing, this for sure was not my signature. I could prove it by showing them how I did sign my name. These guys were out to screw me, I thought, why I had no idea. I started to get angry to think this pair would doubt my word, treat me like a suspect. But my anger mixed with fear. These were NCO lifers, non-commissioned officers who could make my life miserable behind the First Sergeant's back. Feeling my face getting hot, I wavered – but anger won out. I didn't accuse either one. I pressed them to look at my real signature, took a pen and scrawled it out. One of them said,

Waill, shit! How do I know, there's nothing to compare it to – how do I know that ain't forged what you just wrote? At that I almost grinned, but said nothing, and quickly the other corporal elbowed his buddy and said,

C'mon, leave him alone.

I signed a new form for a replacement canteen only, got it and left. It was my first run-in with petty chicanery. I absorbed it as a lesson. It reinforced my loner way and I never forgot it. Those stupid corporals tried the same trick on Philadelphia, and that outcome made me feel good for having resisted, made me wonder why I'd been so timid. Philadelphia, reluctant draftee, answered their trickery with immediate aggressive belligerence: *I didn't lose a thing on bivouac, and that's not my signature, and you guys can just fuck off!*

V
Nostalgia

At a certain point, before announcement of the truce at Panmunjom that summer of 1953, we were called to ranks one evening after chow for a show-and-tell. A much-decorated First Lieutenant back from Korea, awarded the Bronze Star for bravery under fire, was introduced by the First Sergeant himself. This hero was just out of 19 months in hospital and rehab. He was going to speak to the company "first-hand" about what we'd be up against "out there." The text of what he said is gone; at first it was standard patriotic rhetoric about "opposing communist aggression," but gave way to his grim main theme, the reason he was here addressing us. Like all cadre so far, he talked generalities about what we'd be up against in Korea, where most of us would surely be sent.

Those North Korean and Chinese soldiers are formidable enemies, well trained, highly disciplined and numberless, the terrain very rugged and inhospitable, the winters extremely cold. You'll have to stay alert every minute and trust your buddy. You will pass through hell itself. And I can tell you, some of you are going to die there.

And so forth in that vein for some time. The capstone to his performance shocked us. The hero took off his dark green dress uniform blazer, spangled with medals and ribbons and a Combat Infantryman's Badge, then removed his tie and finely-tailored blouse, revealing a powerfully muscled torso beneath a snowy

T-shirt. Then he removed his trousers, to gasps from the ranks. One of his legs was smaller in diameter than his biceps, the other only slightly less scrawny. He had taken at least eight machine gun slugs between pelvis and knees, but had persevered at arms in some manner – he refrained from finishing the story – and lived to tell the tale. There was absolute silence when he began the finishing touch of his performance. He assumed the position and started in, continuing for minutes on end, the First Sergeant counting repetitions out loud, and when it was over the officer had done 110 pushups. Nobody in the company had come anywhere near that number in physical training. I had managed 42. When the performance was over we dispersed, subdued and silent, but I heard guys talking later. This lieutenant, after being wounded, legs useless, had pulled himself forward hand over hand for yards and tossed a grenade into the machine gun nest that had shot him up, thus saving his men pinned down by the gun. So it was said.

Thus training went, ideological as well as "practical." I sloughed off most of the details as I had religion, or maybe they got lost in the fog of perpetual fatigue. There was an attempt to lure us into volunteering for Paratrooper School. We were offered the inducement of "jump pay" if we qualified. You had to be really tough as well as smart to be certified a Paratrooper. Having nothing better to do, I was in the dayroom that evening with three or four other guys, but I focused on the gauntlet of brute labor and risk the recruiter laid before us: unending PT, and you packed your own chute for every jump. Your life was in your hands every time you went out the plane door. It was in character for me to be incapable of such trust in myself, though I'd never been afraid of heights.

Another initiative was a chance to take the test for OCS – Officers Candidate School. The Army generously offered ordinary enlisted GIs the possibility of schooling to make them second lieutenants, officers – if they could cut the mustard. Both of these sessions ocurred close in time, the first conducted by a spit-polished paratrooper sergeant in a steel helmet he'd had chrome-plated at his own expense. He repeatedly emphasized the élite status of paratroopers, but I felt no adventurous stirrings and left the dayroom as soon as I could without seeming rude. The OCS session was much the same. The first lieutenant who conducted it was likewise spit-polished, and talked to us about "command functions, better pay and benefits – the Officers' Club, more prestige" – and here I listened, perhaps even attentively. But I felt and couldn't understand a puzzling resistance to go for it. In my mind I was somehow "on track" right here, never mind the likelihood of being sent to Korea. To take the OCS option seemed a "diversion" but I couldn't specify how that would be so. An extended tour of service was required. Both these recruiting efforts were without deadline – we could think them over and apply any time. The open-endedness let me off the hook – by then I was used to making life decisions by avoiding them. Perhaps I had heard by then that the combat death rate was highest for infantry lieutenants.

Around then I had a dream I didn't understand in any way. It seemed portentous and a fragment of it stayed with and puzzled me for years. In the dream I stood facing a file of men who were slowly turning and walking away from me, one by one. I was watching them leave without comment, merely observing. As the last one turned to go, it seemed to be an officer but I wasn't sure. Speaking in an even and slightly disdainful voice, he said

You're just a common poilu...

I had studied French in high school, enthusiastically but without marked achievement, and almost certainly the word "poilu" was not in my vocabulary. At the time of the dream I didn't even recognize it as French, further mystifying me. Years later, studying French in college, I had an *Aha!* experience: caught up then in the diffuse horror of military dehumanization,

I had so far kept my head low, had indeed striven to be an ordinary foot-soldier, a *poilu*. I never aspired to more. Where that word came from I had no idea, until – years later I thought I understood that in dreams of that kind, *one is talking to one's unconscious.*

Heavy weapons were just that, needing more than one man to carry and load and fire them. Thus began emphasis on closer teamwork than parade-ground drill required. At first, fixing on "adventure," paradoxically I couldn't get enough of them, BARs, mortars heavy and light, machine guns, rocket launchers, recoilless rifles – the list was long and meant treks to distant ranges and thunderous explosions. But it turned out that this was "familiarization" instruction only. I came to see how skimpy the training actually was, how much time and practice were needed to get proficient with these killing machines. Three cartridges each were issued us to learn how a .50-calibre heavy machine gun worked, with the gun plunked down in tall grass with no visible target. Frustrated, I asked a cadreman how to get more practice and was told,

That'll have to wait till you git where you're goin'. His remark chilled me: how casually this Army would send greenhorns into battle! As we marched back to post, I heard the heavy guns open up in sustained bursts, and cynically I figured it was the range crew having fun at our expense.

Predictably, I met the stress of teamwork with difficulty, aware that the various teams I took part in were transitory, which seemed to preclude effectiveness we would need in real combat. We already knew we wouldn't go overseas as a unit. But one of the exercises I found actually gratifying. The heavy machine gun of that time was a behemoth, the gun itself heavy, detachably mounted in a heavy cradle atop a rugged low tripod. The barrel was enclosed by a large cylinder with a plug to fill it with cooling water. The weapon rapidly became hot under continuous fire, and would jam or burn out its barrel if the water jacket wasn't kept full. The instructor told us the story of old Oliver Winchester, back in the 1800s, trying to sell his new repeating rifle to the Turkish government. He was invited to demonstrate the weapon, and it performed well. Then a Turk asked for one and thoroughly dredged it in a nearby mud puddle and handed it back to Winchester, demanding that he shoot it. The enterprising American excused himself, took the rifle a little apart from the group and urinated it clean, then fired it. The Turks laughed uproariously, but bought the rifles, went the story. Quieting our laughter, the instructor said he wasn't in the business of entertaining us but teaching us, and said about this water-cooled machine-gun that we could do the same thing as Oliver Winchester if need be.

So – if you find your gun with an empty water jacket and you have a canteen half-full, for god's sake, save that water to drink!

For this drill we fell into teams of three: gun carrier, mount carrier, ammo handler. The exercise consisted of taking apart a mounted gun on signal, dashing in sequence with the lowest visibility profile to a new position perhaps 50 yards up a bare slope, to remount the weapon and fire a three-round burst in the shortest time. We practiced the maneuver "dry" twice only, and when live-fire competition came, me and two mates found a magical attunement to each other in the performance, like machines, with no wasted motion. We won against the rest of the company. The constant harping on teamwork, on getting a buddy, made sudden sense to me. Eberhard, our *de facto* medic and hitherto the closest I had to a buddy, merely went through the motions.

Finally! A weekend pass to go off post! Even then, the cadre wouldn't let up harassing us. One poor slob failed that Saturday morning inspection because a housefly landed on his shoulder while the inspecting officer stood scrutinizing him.

Disease-bearing insect on left epaulet, said Lieutenant Green, in his mild smiling drawl.

No pass for you, Dawson, said the sergeant. After inspection was over, the officer gone, the sergeant said,

I don' really want to see anybody hangin roun the barracks this afternoon – cept you, Dawson – don worry, you wont get lonely, I got plans for you.

Everybody was going to Henderson, but I waffled about even going to town until there was only one bus possibility left. I couldn't say why I was disinclined. Money? – I probably had some, but not much, in my pocket. Memory is careless with feelings. I remember a jolt of impatience at my ambivalence. Impulsively I grabbed my gold high school ring from the footlocker, pocketed it and ran for the bus. The interval of the trip let me address the matter of hocking the ring. A symbol, the ring stood for something perhaps positive, but I couldn't have said what. I grabbed it without thought. It would have been different had it sported a real ruby: authenticity was real. In the end I decided I had no use for the damned thing – I couldn't wear it in uniform and had no civilian clothes, they were useless here.

In Henderson I hocked the ring for five dollars, the only pawn shop deal I ever made. I bought a half-pint of Old Crow whiskey and a real ice cream cone in a sleepy run-down drug store full of flies. I passed a pile of newspapers headlining another story about this Senator McCarthy raising hell in Washington.

Wondering where my barracks-mates had gone, I sat on a bench on the courthouse square, damp-shirted in the sultry heat. I saw only a few soldiers, trainees like myself, nobody I knew. The dusty shaded square, destitute of women and children, featured silent old men in bib overalls wearing what I thought of as "slouch hats." They sat elbows on knees on iron benches around a Confederate War Memorial, a blackish-green statue of some mounted Rebel hero brandishing a saber from the back of a lunging horse. I couldn't have cared less who this hero was, and started to doze off on the curbstone after the ice cream, the bench having become uncomfortable. The flat bottle was a hard presence in my back pocket. It began to bother me. I didn't know why I'd bought it in the first place except I could do so *legally* in Kentucky at 19. I'd have to hide it on going back to post and realized I didn't want a drink of it. I'd have to hide somewhere to open it and take a swig. It was small enough to smuggle back to barracks. I could carry it inside my hat, this silly flat headgear the guys called "cunt caps" for reasons I was clueless about. Warm, semi-somnolent from the ice cream load, definitely not meditating, the hocked ring floated accusingly in my mind. I sat out that long Saturday afternoon doing absolutely nothing with my first reprieve in months from chickenshit harassment. In a bizarre and inexplicable way I became attached to that forlorn scrap of civic ground which meant absolutely nothing to me.

One of the old men sitting nearby, asked the time by another, dipped into a chest pocket of his worn overalls, took out a small nickel-plated revolver, laid it in his lap, went back in for a pocket watch, opened it, spat a goodly stream of tobacco juice and said the hour, snapped the watch shut and dropped it back in along with the pistol, to resume staring straight ahead. The town of Henderson never entertained me again. I never missed the ring.

VI
A Way Out

My ignorance of the politics of war, of all politics, didn't let me appreciate the subtle distinction of the Korean fighting as a "conflict" rather than a war, as the politicians insisted on calling it. The guys argued about it, about war in general, some declaiming passionately against "godless communism." Philadelphia and others protested the current national paranoia, "this crazy fuckin' domino theory." If the government wanted to defend other people from their neighbors why didn't they consult their own people first, those who would do the bloody work? The notion of greed as a primary war driver underlying the National Interest, whatever that was, was beyond me then.

Philadelphia, I learned when argument spilled over to the Rosenbergs, was totally against the death penalty, against killing for any reason except self-defense. In my gut I silently agreed with him. Keenly self-conscious about my naivety, I didn't participate in political bull sessions often, and was usually uncomfortable listening to others. I acted as if free speech were to be used sparingly, when necessary. Some part of my cloudy thought was entangled with being Regular Army, a volunteer, potentially "professional." Did the oath I'd sworn without God at induction include strictures about political neutrality, the way my father was bound by the Hatch Act? Yet I agreed cautiously when Philadelphia condemned Joe McCarthy as a "fascist threat to freedom" one night. Some guys looked on with the hard eyeballs of profound disagreement. Later there were mutters, erroneous comments about this "pinko Jew" – though Philadelphia was neither one nor the other.

The company had one last live fire exercise to go through. We found ourselves in a skirmish line alongside a dirt road after full dark, wearing battle gear and listening attentively as the sergeant briefed us on what was coming. He spoke in terse generalities, specifying nothing. Sometime back he had teased us with obscure remarks about crawling through machine gun fire.

You men ain't seen nothin to bitch about yet – you just wait, we gotta little surprise waitin for ya.

Evidently this was it – or was it? In the black softness of a damp night we waited, mildly anxious.

You will all go through with this; you will all do it, every mother's son of ya. There will be no, I repeat, no turnin back. Is that clear? Then he put us to crawling on our bellies down a slope, descending into sparse, crackly brush, sharp stones and bitter silky dust, unable to see anything clearly.

Get that butt down, Gaffney!

I found it nearly impossible to cradle the heavy rifle and keep it out of the dirt, protecting it like it was a baby or something, meanwhile getting yelled at to keep moving.

Get that butt down!

I was quickly aware of intensely sensitive knees and elbows. The steel pisspot on my head kept tipping forward to block what little I could see. I came to a deep gully at the apparent foot of the slope, discovering it more by feel than sight, though there was faint starshine. Crossing the gully without standing up would be a challenge. Officers and non-coms were there, hunched over, monitoring the crossing and enforcing the prone position.

As foretold, .30-calibre machine-guns opened up loudly. Even officers flinched at the sudden racketing streams of angry red tracers criss-crossing the black night above our heads. The point of the exercise was to advance on our bellies up the slope beneath the continuous hammering of the guns, meaning we would ascend gradually and inexorably toward the deadly lead lacing this shallow valley. Preoccupied with knees and elbows I was not aware of fear, only of a stern imperative to press myself into the dirt. The sergeant had guaranteed "nothing to worry about if you keep down." Unafraid I relied on his words, actually excited by the fiery chattering streams whose height was impossible to guess.

Then Gaffney of the hand grenade incident was beside me saying he couldn't cross that ditch, he was too short. A corporal urged and then ordered him to try it, but Gaffney shouted that if he got down in the ditch he couldn't climb back out. As I watched, two hunched-over NCOs approached and shouted at him for awhile to no avail. Soon, one on each side, they picked him up by arm and canteen belt and pitched the Pennsylvanian across the gully cursing the while. In order to "help" him they'd had to elevate themselves more than they liked. But that told me the gunfire was well above our heads, at least here in the bottom. Rolling my legs into the ditch, I found it deep but not watery. I gathered myself and by jumping hard, but not too hard, several tries, managed to claw myself out of the gully and stay low doing it. The up-slope going was harder. My progress was too slow for the lieutenant watching over this end of the line. He yelled at me to keep moving. Breathing hard after negotiating the ditch, I waited till the officer moved away. Then I rolled onto my back and rested, watching the crepitating red chatter that seemed only inches above my nose. I thought about that wounded lieutenant who had done 110 pushups.

Inspiration came. Keeping low, I wriggled out of my pack and placed it on my chest and belly along with the canteen on its belt. I clutched everything together using rifle and hands. By arching my neck and back, pushing and kicking with my heels and using my helmet as a skid, I propelled myself in short bursts the remaining yards up the slope, where I lay disoriented by my zigzags and the roar of the guns. Shortly I could make out that I was even with, and between, two of the machine gun emplacements, which continued yammering as if they had all the ammo in the world. Safe now, pack under my head, I rested and enjoyed the spectacle of fiery crashing noise, fascinated by the incandescent red hosing out into the blackness. Occasionally I heard cadre below urging the rest of the platoon forward, and after awhile it was over. The cease fire order was repeated several times before the gunners got it, and then the night was lit by a pair of brilliant flares. Dangling on little parachutes, they revealed the scope and some details of what we'd gone through. The machine guns were on concrete pads, their jacketed barrels poking through rectangular steel bars tightly limiting vertical motion but allowing horizontal sweep. The swale we had crawled into and then out of was almost completely barren, totally denuded, scarified by the mindless harrowing of countless boys at war-play.

I felt general relief when the truce was signed at Panmunjom that July. Morale in the platoon improved noticeably. The cadre seemed to behave with greater leniency, less imperious discipline. There were now magazines and newspapers, old ones, in the dayroom and card games in the barracks at night. At some point we were given access to a sort of beer-garden which however served only three-point-two beer. Weapons training had become show-and-tell, no more hands-on experience. We watched from bleachers as a veteran crew demonstrated a jeep-mounted recoilless rifle. I was spellbound at the unerring hits of high explosive shells on derelict tanks and battered concrete blockhouses in the distance – perhaps built for the purpose.

Training ended almost before we knew it was coming. Sharpshooter medals were given out – even Gaffney got one, what a joke. Then, a final dragged out "graduation" inspection and parade. We waited for orders – *hurry up and wait* – polishing floors, doing KP, standing pointless inspections, drinking

A Way Out

beer in the evening if we had money, which I didn't because a deduction from my pay was now going to my father for the car I'd torn up. But things had eased up. New dentures came which my tough gums almost didn't need. Life was not bad, not like the beginning, only endless waiting to see where in the world we were going. Shooting had seemingly stopped in Korea, a relief to me and probably most of us. The first sergeant, cynical as ever about war and peace, now seemed much more like a human being, ready to talk to us, to shoot the shit.

A cryptic notice appeared on an out-of-the-way bulletin board, in barely readable military lingo, something about "special duty" assignments available, "Stateside only." Interested volunteers were to report to Personnel. I went next morning. The office was not crowded but I got no answers to questions about the nature of these assignments.

What are "Special Weapons"? The Personnel clerk ignored my question, shrugged his shoulders and said bluntly,

Yes or no? – wanting his answer so he could flip the form into a basket and get on to whatever came next. Impulsively I said "Yes," thinking only to avoid Korea. I was glad for his bored disinterest, relieved at not being questioned about my "real" reasons for applying.

No guarantee you'll get this assignment – you'll wait for orders like everybody else.

Hurry up and wait...

Eventually orders were read: 84 of us to Korea, 25 to Europe, Germany mostly and a dozen stateside, including me! When my name was called I sighed in relief. I did not want to go to Korea. Perhaps this would answer my slightly revised hope of being more than just a plain dogface. "Special Weapons." Maybe I would become an "élite soldier," nevermind paratrooper school or OCS. Shortly I got orders to report to a place I'd never heard of, Sandia Base, Albuquerque New Mexico.

Nothing in my life had prepared me to search out beforehand details of determining choices facing me. I was a volunteer; thus intimidated, I did not imagine challenging that Personnel clerk. It was spooky how some cadre reacted when I asked if they knew anything about "Special Weapons." Everyone I questioned professed ignorance but I sensed that some knew more than they were saying but wouldn't tell. I couldn't put my finger on anything and felt misgivings but dismissed them. Life was looking good, in the fulness of what was in fact physical rehabilitation by these sixteen rigorous weeks. Later I couldn't help feeling "special" myself at getting this assignment. There was a delicious if tentative sense of vindication. I felt as if official eyes of extra keenness had spotted me for this program, whatever it was. I weighed more than at any time before or since, with muscle power I would not have thought possible. I could even manage a one-handed pullup on the way in to chow. The accumulated fatigue of the summer drained away. I stood tall, strode rather than walked. In the end, a self-proclaimed atheist who totally rejected faith in favor of grabbing "the main chance," I didn't give a thought to the fact I was blindly trusting the Army – with absolutely no idea what I'd volunteered for.

VII
Sandia

The minutiae of travel orders and transportation are mostly gonefrom memory I was authorized to fly to my new station. The Personnel clerk asked from where I would travel to New Mexico, but I was unable to rise above a jumble of conflict in my breast. I recoiled, perhaps visibly, at the prospect of "going home." The Army was throwing in an ample margin of travel time, not really necessary, plus cash for meals and lodging. There was no real reason to go to Virginia, but what to do with the time until I reported to Sandia? Typically I had given no thought to options and took the default alternative, the clerk waiting for an answer: "Washington National."

Carrying my bulky duffel bag I caught a bus to Henderson, bought a Greyhound ticket and a pint of Old Crow and sunk myself in a rear seat on the battered noisy Road Cruiser as afternoon extruded into a muggy evening. The whiskey was premeditated medication, intended to wall out the rocking drumming roar of the aged bus. I meant to put myself to sleep to avoid thinking about my destination. The trip strung out to twelve hours of anything but true sleep.

Achy and properly hung over, I persuaded the driver to make an unscheduled stop, and emerged into pre-dawn cool at Fairfax Courthouse, the closest point to my father's house without going on to downtown D.C. From a pay phone I called someone, a brother or my father, to pick me up.

The visit was brief. My newest and last sister, Number 14, was a toddler already. My father took a group photograph of the entire family, Grandma included, seventeen people in all. It was the last full family assembly before death began its winnowing. Some of us – maybe all – seemed aware of that.

I left D.C. on a transcontinental non-stop flight aboard a TWA Constellation, the finest plane of its time, a vibrating pressurized prop job that delivered me into brilliant pale desert edged by green mountains that evening, joints aching from the trip. Coming off the plane I seemed to float in a soft-focus aura mingling excitement, fatigue, anticipation. I had lied in departing a day earlier than my orders called for. Exercising shaky self-conscious autonomy, money in my pocket, I went downtown from the airport by cab and took a room in the Franciscan Hotel. After a shower and a meal I bought a newspaper with yet another story about the Rosenberg execution weeks before, and having spoken to no one since my goodbyes that morning, I commented on the story to the hotel desk clerk.

Oh, yes, I read that this morning – they stayed here, y'know, maybe even your room. What room are you? Oh yes, fourteen. I'm pretty sure the Rosenbergs stayed in that room – or maybe nearby.

I suffered mildly disturbed sleep that night, caught in gloomy musing on the definition of treason and the awful penalty. In the morning I wondered how execution remedied anything. My unease, in some vague familiar way, seemed detached from the executions; I decided it was due to the novelty of this new situation, a stranger in a strange land.

Reporting to the base, I showed my orders and asked an MP for directions. The building was a large concrete block several stories high with big bays at the ends of long hallways lined with smaller rooms. Some listless men were on hand. We exchanged names and a few handshakes. I briefly answered the inevitable "Where you from?" I picked out a bunk, got info from the others, went down to Supply, drew bedding and a footlocker, and unpacked my duffel bag. Then began weeks or months of weightless limbo, how long I know not, waiting for just what nobody knew. "Await further orders."

Military secrecy was thick in the air and showed itself in brusque barbed wire and chainlink fencing everywhere. I saw compounds doubly ringed, the inner one electrified. Armed MPs were seldom absent in any field of view. But I felt the weight of secrecy most heavily in the demeanor of inhabitants of this walled and ringed military stronghold next to the old city of Albuquerque. Distant looks on bland faces, eyes almost but not quite averted seemed to lack a certain animus. Routine necessary expression seemed ruled by measured vocal penury almost dreamlike, as if something delicate had evaporated from routine workaday speech:

I need new boots.
Quartermaster's three blocks up on the right.

As time passed I had feelings of somehow recognizing myself in these people I found myself among, feeling a general "opacity" around them that was merely puzzling, not quite sinister. Greenhorn and a loner, I thought I could detect "subtle pretense" in their bearing and speech, as if obliged to play-act sentience and self-control even while guided by some invisible force-field, the "pretense" seeming to mean they knew precisely what they were doing at this time, in this place.

On the surface the base seemed to be run rather informally, even casually. No officers or non-coms bothered or seemed interested in me. Seldom did anyone salute an officer. One captain anticipated my telegraphed intent and half-heartedly waved off the formality. This was a "holding company," and we were outside looking in, our entry pending. Me and my new bunkmates stood roll call every morning, then were dispatched to wax this or that hallway, or assigned to police the parade ground of butts, or report for KP. We isolates soon found ways to dodge make-work duty, KP excepted. Yet we were not disciplined when caught goofing off. After awhile I discovered footlockers of well-thumbed paperback books in the dayroom. I fell to and was soon devouring a collection of "shoot-em-up" Westerns, ignoring the Agatha Christies and Erle Stanley Gardners in favor of Max Brand, Louis Lamour, Zane Grey. Other newcomers drifted in, settled down and found the books. After the grinding lockstep of basic, this life was almost cushy.

Eventually we were given interrogatory forms to list our life histories for an FBI background check. This event caused a mild flurry of gabble in the bays, speculation about the nature of Sandia Base and what it was all about. The FBI form was "head work." Its perjury warning spun me briefly toward Catholic confession mode, but life soon slipped back to routine boredom. Our menial duties gave us something to bitch about, and we did. After all, we were supposed to be some unspecified cut above plain GIs, chosen for some kind of Special Duty.

Free to leave base after hours, guys went downtown evenings, returning late, but on my first sally I was carded underage and denied admission to a night club. I didn't leave post again for a long time. Penny-ante poker became an evening pastime. Six-packs of real beer snuck in from time to time. Boredom soon blanketed the bay, wearing at us. Fidgety acting-out began to interrupt endless days of sterile moil which was and was not drudgery.

Those were the boom days of megalomaniacal military fantasies as the Cold War indulged in its ravening. One of the wildest dreams was the B-36 bomber based at adjacent Kirtland Air Force Base. The largest propeller-driven plane ever built, it had six engines on the trailing edge of enormous droopy wings. Allegedly a fighter plane hung in its belly, to be dropped when needed from the bomb bay, to unfold wings and take flight to defend the "mother" ship. This behemoth was flying regularly out of Kirtland. The crescendo of its interminable takeoff run brought it directly over our barracks. Its earth-shaking passage obliterated talk and set "Lucky Lager" cans thrumming toward the edge of our footlocker card table. Every time I heard one coming I tried to get to a window to see the damned thing. Weeks went by before I got a clear view and I was properly awed by its enormity, but shortly I came to resent its thunderous disrupting passage.

As with any group of adolescents left unattended or purposeless for long, morale began to deteriorate. We were an assorted lot from various parts of the country, young innocents mostly accepting of each others' quirks except for one midwesterner of morose disposition and plodding ways always called "Private Barry." His depressive mien was quickly recognized. He seemed to shower infrequently and the entire bay came to dread the moment when he took off his boots for sleep. Once it was clear that the spreading fetor correlated to his bedtime behavior, guys discussed the situation in angry or sarcastic tones. No one addressed Private Barry directly. Eventually there was talk of giving him a shower "whether he needed one or not." Nothing was done however, no leader emerging. Heckling by some in nearby bunks continued from time to time, but I merely avoided him.

On a Sunday night with no cadre around, three guys with a car got some cherry cider, threw a blanket over a footlocker and started a card game. I joined them, and when the gallon jug was half gone its owner brought forth a fifth of vodka and poured it in. Later he did likewise with the other jug. We were soon roaring drunk, ignoring protests from disgruntled "teetotalers" trying to sleep. The poker game broke down and the claque degraded into mournful bitching on the theme "This fucking Army has fuckin forgot we fuckin exist!" Next morning I could barely stand still for reveille. When the brief formation was over I rushed around the corner of the building, the organism desperate to throw off self-inflicted poisoning. I wasn't alone in the racking misery of my "dry heaves."

Meanwhile bureaucratic plans were congealing. We began to encounter more officers on the ground floor headquarters. Obliquely observant, I gradually became aware that a battalion was forming in our midst. One day a sergeant appeared whom nobody knew. He was informal and talkative, a congenial lifer who had seen combat action in WW2. He said vaguely we'd be seeing more of him in coming days.

Why we gonna see more of you?

Sarge, what the hell is goin on around here? We don't know a damn thing!

But the sergeant wouldn't say anything specific, only that he'd been assigned here. We would learn more when the new outfit was "up to strength." He ticked off some names, non-coms, warrant officers, and commissioned officers already known to us who would be part of the outfit. A few days or weeks later this same Logan told me over coffee I was sure to get a security clearance since I was young and had never been arrested. Then he referred obliquely to the "school" we'd be going to but would say no more.

Better wait till your clearance comes through. This Sergeant Logan was shorter than me, at least twice my age, with a big nose and warm brown eyes. He laughed easily for a lifer, but when nothing was going on his face settled into wan moroseness.

Late one night I was roused by fervent disputation at the other end of the bay. The voices were not loud, but strong emotions were unmistakable. I strained to hear over Private Barry's snoring, but I couldn't make out anything clearly. I recognized one of the speakers, Bob Manning from Michigan, but unable to follow what was being said, and having no interest in butting in, I drifted back to sleep. The following evening there was palpable tension in the bay when I came back from chow. An argument was in progress: Bob Manning, beset by three guys. I heard words about patriotism, communism, about following orders no matter what, heard Manning's repeated rejoinder,

I won't do it, no matter what; this is a free country. Everybody had serious, even grim expressions. I asked Tucker, passing by, what was going on.

You haven't heard? Christ, I thought everybody knew; Manning wants to go to Korea.

Korea? What in hell for?

Got me – says over there, it'd be his decision to kill somebody or not.

But the war's over...

Yeah, maybe; but maybe not...

It don't make sense; why would a guy want out of this kind of duty to go back to the infantry?

Ask him – it's plumb disgusting...

What d'ya mean?

Well, shit, he's just a crybaby – says he can't stand the thought of messing around with atomic weapons, says he doesn't want to learn a single thing about 'em. Thinks he's better'n us, I reckon...

What you mean, atomic weapons? I was suddenly on full alert.

Geez, where the hell you been? We're going to school to work on special weapons.

Atomic weapons – bombs?

They got all kinds, even howitzer shells...you didn' know?

Where indeed had this simple shit been? My reaction to the revelation after weeks of hang-fire speculation was high excitement. But I dissembled and said mildly,

Well, I didn't think they were talking about "toys" when they said "Special Weapons."

This tale is a tedious tracery, disordered betimes. An unclean bend in the wandering twists of the spoor conjugates with dreamtime, of which I was then already susceptible, though unwittingly.

A certain *Atom Bomb Ring* had been advertised on a cereal box long before I left home, a premium offered by *WHEATIES the Breakfast of Champions*. Detail about its acquisition is gone. My Mom's sketchy diary provides clues to when it happened. I begged her for the coins to enclose in the envelope. The ring was some ad man's idea of what an atom bomb looked like, bluntly pointed nose, body fat and slightly tapering, perhaps five eighths of an inch long, with four short fins at the rear where a tiny lens was inset. One squinted into it, a darkened room was advised, and after eyes accomodated to night vision, one could see an occasional infinitesimal twinkle, an "atomic reaction" in tiny flashes so brief I wasn't quite sure something had happened. But persisting in squinting long and hard, eventually I saw the fugitive glints: single photons?[1] I have no idea what went through my rapt mind as I stared into the mysterious talisman?

When Hiroshima and Nagasaki were blasted we were living in Virginia then. A fleeting but indelible visual persists: the scene is Maple Street, nearly empty and stretching away in drowsy late afternoon heat. There is an audio track, a chance-heard broadcast reporting the awful annihilation, from a store owner's radio wafting out an open window. After the sensational report ends, I am walking on toward home like an automaton, gripped as if by rigid and invisible forceps clamped around my neck from behind. I am governed by a ghastly feeling I never felt before, infinitely worse than when my father took off his belt. Was I holding onto, perhaps *wearing* that breakfast cereal atomic icon as the awful broadcast gripped me? The horror, with no physical sequelae following, waned after a while.

The ring was sinister enough, but with the nuclear braggadocio of the press, it had credibility as convincing as specious – except to an 11-year old. I stared intently into its rear end. Possibly I would have echoed that I was glad "we" had the real bomb and not Hitler or Tojo. (Stalin was not yet broadly projected onto the common mind as a monster.) Can "serendipity" cover horrific as well as beatific experience? Would I have wound up at Sandia Base in fall 1953 had my Mom refused the two quarters and a stamp to send away for an Atom Bomb Ring? Was that malignant bauble connected in some way with my arrival at the heart of nuclear barbarity? I could never accept that Japanese people were "subhuman" as one read in the newspaper. Sam did so when I got to know him, calling them "fuckin animals." If I did succumb to the demonizing around me – it is possible – its traces have not survived, perhaps overshadowed by Hitler and the SS monstrosities.

It was soon apparent that many of my barracks-mates felt strongly negative about Manning's decision to seek a transfer, which Headquarters let him know meant inevitably "Infantry, Korea." Some guys said he was yellow, an outright coward, a chicken-liver. Manning had had no idea what this outfit was up to and was horrified to hear what "Special Weapons" were. He wanted out before he learned a thing about them. He didn't know if the Army would give him a transfer but said even if they court-martialled him he would not go to Special Weapons School. He was a draftee sent here straight out of basic. He had not volunteered for this duty and did not like it.

Scuttlebutt had it that even though a truce had been signed at Panmunjom, shooting was still going on and might continue a long time. These were Chinese Communists after all, numberless and fanatically tenacious. It was far from clear that the war was really over. But Manning stubbornly held to his position and went to headquarters regularly to see about his status. Guys continued to harass him scornfully, but others said, perhaps falsely, that they were concerned for him.

Forget it! said Manning, *I know what I'm doing and why. Your concern is misplaced – you should be concerned with yourselves, you dumb shits, wanting to play around with this atomic stuff. At least with a rifle, I'd have some choice about pulling the trigger. You mess with these bombs and you'll be killing people, civilians, anonymously, in great numbers, and I can't take that.*

The wrangling resulted in ostracizing of Manning by some. I did not actively offer him support, but stayed away from the badmouthing. He got his transfer before weapons school started. His argument disturbed me, made me "wonder about things" – but feebly. I was unable to dwell on it for long, making no connection to abstract notions of "duty" or "love for country." Priding myself on my "skeptical turn of mind," yet there remained things one simply did automatically without thought, expressions of values I had not the imagination to question. "Service" was such an abstraction, distasteful to hold in my mind. Yet my difficulty dealing with the notion indicated it was part of my makeup, though I would have denied so. It was a long time before I saw my patriotic volunteerism as gullible assent to the beck and call of Power. I couldn't glimpse the reality Manning talked of, certainly could not foresee the effect on my psychic future of blindly grabbing this brass ring to avoid infantry duty in Korea.

On impulse I approached Manning privately in the hallway one afternoon and said I admired his guts for "taking all this heat from those jerks." I wished him well going overseas.

Well, said Manning, *I'm surprised at you, wanting to get mixed up in this stuff. I was drafted, and I don't mind serving my time, but this is too much. But you actually volunteered for this, and I can't understand that. I know you know what it means and yet you're still gonna do it.* He shook his head and went on.

There it was in stark terms: this man thought it was worth catching a sniper's bullet in Korea – or worse – to refuse involvement in atomic warfare, which after all was only hypothetical. Americans didn't go around bombing innocent civilians, notwithstanding Hiroshima and Nagasaki, unmentioned. And likely none of us knew that MacArthur had advocated "dosing" the Chinese on their side of the Korean border with 20 or 30 atom bombs to bring them to their knees and make a real end to the war.

In a few more days it turned out that Manning had converted another draftee, Dave Branch who, seeing what Manning was put through, had kept his mouth shut about applying for transfer. He revealed it only as he packed his duffel bag, saying to no one and everyone,

Manning was right, you know – this Army's a whole different ball game.

There's no documentary evidence, only nebulous shreds of memory about my state of mind in swallowing hook, line and sinker whatever the Army had in store for me. Debate the issue I did, internally, though I never got near the nut of the decision to make war in Korea, the reasons for it. Rather I maundered over it, caught in murky self-flagellating nonverbal circularity, unable to articulate "pro" or "con." I cautiously avoided taking sides for or against Manning's strong view – for which he had openly repudiated any religious basis. In the still of the night after Branch had likewise been returned to the infantry and sent to Korea, I was sleepless, turning over and over in nagging discomfort about "the" – not "my" – situation. With guys snoring around me I could not form an opinion on my own hook. Incapable of owning the problem, I writhed in metaphysical pain; perhaps sheer mental fatigue led me finally to resolve my turmoil.

I sipped the poison. In an almost physical sense I located a seed of something very like self-satisfaction at being where I was, and dwelt on a curious, pleasurable sense of self-gratification. I allowed it to grow. Simultaneously, I was not at all "gung ho" in my mind. I never felt an impulse toward the "thrill of combat," the orgiastic pleasure in killing admitted to by J. B. S. Haldane that jarred me uncomfortably when I read it in college. But on that restless night I could not have named my feelings as "thanksgiving," let alone "peace of mind" or even "good luck."

Yet relief from misery came, which I found almost warm; I soon slept. I could not have verbalized it. Instantly and reflexively touchy about anything smacking of "spirituality," I would have vociferously repudiated anyone who said I was putting my life in the hands of angry gods. But it must be said that my confused mind, observant and already developing an affinity for a well-turned phrase, had seized on the words spoken by J. Robert Oppenheimer as he witnessed the first atomic test at Trinity Site: *Now I am become Death, the Destroyer of Worlds.* I felt something dark and inexpressible in his words, a ghostly horror made real to my ignorance by the brilliant reputation of this co-parent of bombs I would soon work on. My fascination with the remark seems prescient because it was *recursive*, a completed communication. I didn't know for years that Oppenheimer had quoted ancient sacred scripture, whether he did it sardonically or from his heart.

    The Army would have given a Regular Army volunteer a harder time than the two draftees, but I certainly had the same option as Branch and Manning, to seek transfer. In the end I remained at Sandia by choice – "avoiding making waves" is a choice. Eventually we were granted "Q clearances," said to be the highest kind there was. I had been chosen! Not even the President had a higher clearance. There were of course other infinitely imbricated levels of clearance informal and formal, as well as the gauzy doctrine of "need to know." Never mind. I was inside now. I was shown mimeographed orders granting the clearance, individualized with my name only and was not given a personal copy "for security reasons," the battalion clerk said. I had no trouble accepting the secrecy. It seemed to put a seal on the notion that this was Important Stuff and I was now part of it. Later I thought *if this is all a huge mistake,* as Branch and Manning had warned, *it's only for three years – I can take it.*

VIII
Special Weapons

Look at this boy, stuffing yet more woe, putting it aside for a troubled future – of which he could no longer quite claim to be unwitting. I file through a gated opening in electrified chainlink fence, wearing freshly starched fatigues, trousers properly bloused over shiny boots. I sport a new photo ID badge clipped, on instruction of Sergeant Logan to the right pocket flap of my fatigue jacket, in line with other private soldiers. A burly MP stands at the door of the bulletproof gatehouse. Authority straps him with a shiny Sam Brown belt suspending a holstered .45. He wears a security badge of his own. Taking hold of my badge the guard looks keenly at the staring 19-year-old face represented on the plastic card and scans it against the alert flesh before him. Seeming reluctant, he nods barely perceptibly and I pass in with a feeling of "inner sanctum," tingling slightly, senses super-keen, noticing, in the few seconds before something blocks the view, the glassed-in guard tower topping the lethal wire of the enclosure. And then we private soldiers are piled up at a door, waiting to enter a cavernous auditorium with a large projection screen. We sit in comfortable cinema-style seats, murmuring, involuntary hushed tones, a parody of reverence. Our subdued behavior may reflect prehistoric archetypal sacred days and nights in Altamira. But what we are up to is far from mystical communion with the Other, it is initiation of quite another sort.

The Army got through the horrendous part quickly, shots of the ravaged cities that told everything but nothing. Then, repeated soundless slow-motion Technicolor film clips: a sustained blaze of white light on the screen slowly and redly fades into endless billows of mushroom clouds, everything told off with dry statistics: "kilotonnage" and "damage zones" and later, abstract factual material on light, heat, blast and radiation. Later still, we listened to abstruse recitations on "chain reaction" and "critical mass." The terrible names "Hiroshima" and "Nagasaki" were not omitted, but evoking those unimaginable scenes was left to individual imagination. After that, there was never an official whiff of the consequences of nuclear holocaust on *people*; the military lexicon does not contain that language. The officer on stage – we would call him a "presenter" today – spoke blandly and matter-of-factly, revealing no Top Secret stuff as he folded us into our new milieu, warping us toward new meanings of SOP, Standard Operating Procedure. He did not forget to mention the extreme importance of the *Uniform Code of Military Justice* and underlined it with a crisp reference to the Rosenbergs. Starting now, he said, we must carry no written notes out of the room. He suggested we need not even take notes. Pens and pencils went back into pockets. This training would be neither detailed nor comprehensive. Appropriate technical manuals would be available when, finished with this school, we were assigned to the field.

On successive days of alternating lectures and hands-on experience, we saw nuclear "devices" assigned to all three services, from the 280mm artillery projectile with the same "yield" as the Hiroshima bomb, to the long Navy bomb designed to penetrate bedrock-deep Russian sub pens. Its foot-thick cylindrical body was of tungsten carbide, carved and carveable only with diamonds. A peculiar vignette remains from those days of familiarization: myself in the company of a "Fat Man," the plutonium bomb dropped on Japan. Why should we be learning about this gross ugly prototype, almost an antique, six feet in diameter?

Was it just passive show-and-tell of how far development had gone eight years later?

But when we got down to it, the work was more than show-and-tell. Our operations were not conceptually different from the work of car mechanics. We handled the heavy devices, manipulated them, hoisted them onto work stands, disassembled them, acquainted ourselves with general configuration and operation, proceeding from the simple to the complex, ending up at length with an Air Force bomb, the Mark 6 Mod 7, a streamlined dart 10 or 12 feet long, thirty inches in diameter, with three aluminum fins fletching the tail, one of these retracting to make a snug fit under the wing of the fighter plane delivering it. Its warhead we would spend months working with. It was not the highest technology of its time. The cutting edge in 1953 was already thermonuclear.

The Mark 6 was designed for "lob-bombing." The plane releases the weapon at high speed to sail through the air perhaps for miles while its deliverer turns tail and flees. Lob-bombing practice was SOP for jet jockeys. High accuracy was claimed for pilots skilled by sufficient practice throwing training dummies. I happened to look up at a rising jet fighter from Kirtland one day and recognized the unique shapes hanging twinned beneath the wings, and understood why the Mark 6 Mod 7 was called a *tactical* weapon, for use in closer quarters, as was the 280mm artillery round. I mentioned my sighting to my buddies; one replied,

Yeah – any day now they'll issue us nuclear rifle rounds – you shoot and there's a flash and a little mushroom cloud, and when the smoke clears the enemy's been vaporized.

I didn't join the round of guffaws ignited by the joke; I remember a cold, distant feeling lasting seconds before I fumbled to rejoin chow line banter. My chill response was not conscience; Christians owned that word. Later, mentioning my sighting to Sergeant Logan, the crew chief brushed off my report with a comment about "drop tanks" – disposable fuel tanks carried by combat fighters. But this boy was a keen observer. I knew what I'd seen. Jets leaving Kirtland flew low overhead. I began to watch them and often saw Mark 6s, could diagnose the third fin, invisible because of retraction. Drop tanks didn't have fins. These planes were carrying Mark 6s for sure. I wondered, are those live weapons, or dummies for bombing practice?

Initially we worked on dummy warheads, complete in every particular except that the high explosive was replaced with concrete and the inner nuclear sphere substituted with lead. I listened avidly and attentively to technical lectures I could barely understand, stuff about criticality, chain reaction, neutron clouds. An arcane but important distinction existed between detonation and explosion. The black powder we had made as boys could in fact detonate. I recalled Derek's accident when a can of black powder went off in his hand, *detonated*. This was a mysterious process, involving something called "physical chemistry." It was not mere rapid combustion as when a gun goes off; it was qualitatively different. The "HE", or high explosive used in the Mark 6, was known to detonate with a light blow, even to go off while burning passively in the open. Heavy, with a soapy feel, it was fickle stuff – sometimes you could shoot it with a rifle and not detonate it, they said, merely shatter or pierce it. It was enormously more powerful than TNT. High reliability of result, we learned, was obtained with special detonators of great power. On the Mark 6, thirty-odd of these are spaced geometrically around the sphere, fastened into holes in the aluminum encasing the warhead. The detonators press closely against the HE and fire simultaneously when a massive electrical charge vaporizes the fine silver wire on their face. The resulting implosion blasts outer plutonium onto the inner central ball of plutonium, instantly causing criticality and the nuclear "event" in time too quick to measure. Nobody had measured a nanosecond yet in those analog days. Thus it was not possible to ascertain what happened in the event process. The engineers speculated, made hopeful changes, tested them, erred, and tried again, blowing up Nevada in the process. In its dense obscurity it was miraculous to me. I frequently had the sensation of standing next to something terribly important but forever unknowable. Sometimes I saw myself as if I hovered, in a subtle strange state I would never have called "mystical." Neither was it fear, at least not unambiguously. I was often aware of a faint, near-subliminal thrumming sensation within my body: subconscious psychic strain, passionate curiosity and abysmal ignorance grappling with the incomprehensible. In such moments I felt isolated and utterly alone, *alien*. But I felt as well a bizarre thrill I could not articulate. There seemed to mingle with, coexist with dread, a macabre suspicion that behind this horrendous engine of death and destruction was something else, something I could almost but not quite let myself call "beauty." Nothing in these cold hard-edged surroundings spoke to the least degree of anything beautiful. At such moments, Yardley might remind me of a detonator Record Card to fill out; my feelings vanished. Our mission was to turn all this effort into ordinary mundane routine.

And we came close to doing it, joking about last night at the beer garden, while paying close the attention to mechanical detail so deeply installed in blue-collar American males, tightening a bolt to specified foot-pounds or wiping grease with fragrantly sweetish trichlorethylene – said by Logan to "rot your liver" if you inhaled enough of it. Decades after the Army, the physical configuration of the Mark 6 is clear and lives in my memory.

The antiseptic precision, the crisp sheen of tool marks on spotless bright metal machined to a tolerance of a ten-thousandth part of an inch; the opulent gold-plated electronics; the abstractly neuronal bundles of wiring harness; the futuristic Nickel-Cadmium batteries cocooned in self-powered heaters to keep themselves warm during the baleful descent, all this intricate, not quite watchlike detail appended to a heavy industrial construct packed into a package not at all huge but with few cubic inches to spare. This fiendish engine came from another world which we had to make our world. The choreographed moves of the crew, supervised by Mr. Yardley, newly-minted Warrant Officer, gradually congealed into a routine *modus operandi* we followed religiously, with non-judgmental correction when errors were made, which happened from time to time, for we were youngsters. Team members switched roles to become familiar with all; the work protocol was consistent from team to team. Watch us wheel the olive-drab caisson into the work-bay and position it under the hoist. We unseal, unbolt and remove the arched steel cover, gently remove the flat steel case of touchy detonators, gather round to unlatch the curved rhombs of aluminum skin, bring down the hoist hook, attach the lift bracket, raise the awful thing high enough to place a work-stand under it, lower and secure it to the steel with bolts, detach and raise the hoist hook out of the way. Then we go for coffee and a smoke.

What does the thyrotron do exactly, Sarge? I mean, how does it work?

I dunno, don't matter, it works. That's all I know, and if it don't, then we're all in big trouble.

Logan, avuncular old-timer, guarded his coffee break carefully, refusing to let shop talk intrude: break was break, work was work. I never understood the electronic angle of Mark 6 operation. But we soon grasped the sequence of events following release of the bomb from the aircraft. Should the plane be shot down before release, there would be no nuclear event, perhaps only an HE explosion, they said.[2] The two plutonium components were held apart until blasted into the critical mass. I felt deficient as a technician and could only vaguely conceptualize how the electrical discharge touched off the detonators. Daydreaming, remembering sour time spent in my father's thrall while the old man rambled on about vacuum tube diodes or whatnot, all of it rolling off my back even as I said "Unh-huh" while dwelling on squirrel hunting or the new girl over on Locust Street, whose name is gone but not her soft, round form and appealing bosom.

NiCad batteries, state-of-the-art then, powered the process. When the bomb is dropped, switches operate with fiendish ingenuity, energizing it, arming it. Now it is a ponderous teardrop sailing through the unsuspecting ether; the mechanism progresses through a cascading sequence to bring it to the moment: the final lens of high explosive inserts itself on jack-screws like a watermelon plug into its precisely-mated cavity, completing the explosive shell around the plutonium. The same HE plug projects before it the central glob of plutonium, the "cone assembly," a chromium-clad pellet of neutron-rich cobalt at center. Now fully armed and beyond human recall, it follows its breathtaking trajectory with accelerating speed, a nuclearly fertile ovum of annihilation, the mysterious virile thyrotron clenching, building up a massive charge ready to blow detonators when the nose-cone radar finds the target altitude pre-set by human will, upon which it flowers into the inhuman starburst for which there are no words to tell – unless they be Japanese.

Military lore like any other swirls out of jovial hot air among expansive comrades; stories perhaps apocryphal, often unattributable, get swapped around playfully, or outrageously embellished in loud repartée or the half-witted chitchat of boredom. Some stories arise perhaps from carefully dissembled concern for one's own well-being, laughter covering inner tension perhaps not recognized.

Atomic war-making lore was well-developed by 1953, less than a decade after the Trinity shot. The "collegial" Sandia environment was the right place for nuclear anecdotes. I had never heard of AFSWP, the Armed Forces Special Weapons Program, the joint military outfit running Sandia. Having never heard of "interservice rivalry," I never thought twice about all the different uniforms. AFSWP's mission was to parcel out the nuclear inventions of Sandia Labs and Los Alamos to the eager services. We knew nothing about "Pantex," over in Amarillo, Texas.

Early on we passed around the story of the Los Alamos scientist Louis Slotin, unidentified for years, holding a heavy chunk of plutonium aloft on a screwdriver inserted in a hole in the material. On the lab bench was more plutonium and the man was said about to demonstrate "critical mass" to unidentified onlookers, probably other scientists. As Slotin incrementally brought his piece near the other, ticking Geiger counters began to sing, ratcheting through staccato buzzing to a sizzling song. And then the accident happened: he lost control of the dense chunk. It swung or fell near its mate on the bench and everyone in the room was bathed in the blue glow of the neutron / electron cloud universally called "eerie." Stunned, the man jerked his piece away, laid it on the bench and announced that he had just signed his own death warrant – which indeed happened, after days of hideous torture the story went, denied painkillers so that Medicine could get its first "pure" case history of acute radiation poisoning.[3] Other onlookers – their numbers perhaps inflated – died as well, or became perilously sick, lost hair, skin, gut linings and blood.

This story had no specific moral for the boys and men of the 14th Ordinance Battalion (Special Weapons), newly designated, for there was no accidental way for us to replicate the catastrophe in the course of our work. At the time we never learned the name of the dead scientist, and of course heard no credible, complete account of the incident, for face-saving reasons – but political and military ones as well.[4] The medical information provided by other unnamed victims was no doubt useful to selected inhabitants of the dark but ultimately permeable secrecy cloaking the metastatic Manhattan project cancer.

Special Weapons

In a similar vein was the tale of a bunker full of foreign military brass brought to Mercury site in Nevada to witness a test shot. The visitors were seated below ground, their backs toward Ground Zero against a concrete wall some feet thick. Instructed not to jump up and look at the fireball through thick ground-level windows, they were told to wait until the blaze of light on the rear wall started to wane, otherwise their retinas could be burnt despite dark goggles. The shot went off, the blast rocked the bunker and they did as told. Then all rose excitedly and turned to observe the mushroom cloud – except one man, said to be a Japanese colonel, who remained seated. In a few seconds, noticing him, his comrades of the day spoke but got no answer. The man was dead, eyes open, a faint smile on his face. The back of his head had been flattened by the whip of the concrete wall from the blast wave. He had braced himself by pressing his head against the wall: an additional Japanese victim.

I hungered for morbid detail in these sketchy stories and listened intently, my head full of unanswerable questions. What did that poor bastard think about in his terminal torture? And why was a Japanese even there in Nevada? It was not in the nature of these grim tales to be comprehensive or accurate. Similar stories were interlarded with the military counterpart of "medical humor," and sometimes I could laugh at a sick joke floating up at the beer hall, like the unpopular crew boss who grabbed his lunch pail on the way out at noon – and had his shoulder nearly dislocated, some unknown wag having replaced his sandwiches with lead bricks used to shield the cone assembly during operations. And we laughed long about the asinine "Air Farce" officer mortified when a Fat Man broke loose from its canvas-covered trailer, rolled off the road and down a grade while being towed somewhere. The hapless, panicky lieutenant tried to re-conceal the bulky weapon *with his field jacket* – Fat Man was six feet in diameter. Our grim humor – like that corny atomic rifle round – played against and held at bay true metaphysical dread, the real subtext of this hideous game in which we were new players. Our sometimes harsh jocosity functioned to let us stave off looking straight at what we were doing. My own laughter was often superficial. If I did not enter the irreverent repartée more often, it was partly because the natural laugh reflex was long depauperate in me, stunted early in life. But also, just perhaps, our hellish mission was somehow more real to me than to my mates – sometimes.

Early in training I found myself practicing first basics on a dummy Fat Man. We bantered about how "primitive" was this beast, huge, heavy and unwieldy, so big it barely fit into the bomb bay of the B-29 that had dropped one on Nagasaki. Fat Man, an old antique, did not evoke our serious interest in dealing with it. We did more or less only what the dog-eared mimeographed manual required. One afternoon, with Sarge gone, perhaps to the dentist, I stood before its nose, peering into the dark cavity of the outer nuclear sphere, no cone assembly present. Protocol said the inner surface of the spherical cavity was to be swabbed clean with solvent, to remove any scaly radioactive decay products that may have accumulated. From outside I couldn't see or reach inside well enough to do the task correctly. Alone, musing on how best to follow protocol, with neither guidance, supervision nor company, on a zany impulse I took off my boots and climbed into the cavity, wiped the upper and fore "ceiling" of the sphere with a rag damp with the aromatic solvent. I became woozy in the confined space. I exited light-headed and went for fresh air, and full of myself for my "initiative." And I relished a sudden thought: I now had a story for posterity: I've been inside an atomic bomb.

On the job I was mostly cheerful but serious, tending more toward close focus than frivolity, trying to do my best – at least when others were watching. At 19, with no life-focus, I saw only a limited range of work and play options and opportunities. I learned to be disingenuous about work lest my mates accuse me of "bucking for stripes," and in those moments, pain disregarded, I felt again the hated weight of expectations put on me as first-born son. Damn them; I was doing something on my own with my life, was indeed becoming acculturated. Self-centered to a fault, the unaddressed pain I carried into the Army still burned and reawakened with every letter from Grandma. I kept it well stuffed, always in subconscious search mode. I never initiated the merciless humor of those nihilistic days. I might laugh along with others' grotesque ribaldry, but my mind quickly returned to self-involvement. With no call for true initiative in the work bay – I was just a private soldier – I quested for "openings" I knew not what they were, sniffed for opportunity small or large to which I oriented as a sunfish swivels to a dangled worm. Whatever I hungered for, it was somewhere else, beyond me, out in the world somewhere. I oscillated between loneliness and periodic euphoric certainty that if I paid these necessary dues I'd inevitably find "it," failing to notice that this reactive thinking, equally far from atheism as from real thought, merely replicated in secular terms the bizarre notion of "salvation," the spiritual El Dorado at the root of Christian belief.

IX
Spies

The new Battalion comprised three companies. I was assigned to Company A, mission specialists; the other two were B Company, security – MPs; and the brass, the paper-pushers, Headquarters Detachment.

One morning the Company Clerk said,

You won't need yours today, referring to the security badge I collected before going off to weapons school with the guys.

Oh? – how come?

Headquarters is shorthanded today, need a jeep driver this morning. Go see Lieutenant Andrews. And after lunch you're to go down to Building 208 and report to Major Grieden, one o'clock.

What's that about?

Beats me, I'm just telling you what I was told to.

The driving detail was a taxi gig, chauffering Andrews from meeting to meeting with much waiting in between. I'd never driven a jeep before, which made it interesting. The peppy vehicle evoked cowboy impulses that fat-assed old Dodge never did. But my mood was dampened by the enigmatic summons – the guys in the line had stared at me oddly when the clerk gave me the order.

Building 208 was obviously one of the original buildings at Sandia: an almost-humble single-story warren of cubicles made of pine lumber, nails and glass, painted yellow years before. Up three steps to the main entryway, a corridor across the front connecting side-by-side offices. There was apparently nobody in the dusty place. My boots rang the floor hollowly as I searched, slowly, beginning to think I'd screwed up somehow. But all at once there was a Major in fatigues sitting behind a desk that seemed too small for him, facing the door with the nameplate "Grieden" on it. I straightened up, tense, saluted and said,

Private Ellis reporting as ordered, sir.

The major returned more a wave than a salute and said,
Yes, come in. Have a seat.

There was one extra hardbacked chair and nothing on the desk but a clipboard. The Major returned to it, writing steadily as if nothing had happened. Minutes dragged by, the officer totally absorbed in his scriptural endeavor. I was mystified but alert. Was this disciplinary? Had I done something? I had no way to get a handle on this aberrant scene. I had a quick sensation of being somehow still a civilian. Major Grieden had apparently forgotten me. A fly buzzed in a window. Eventually I parked my tension. This was something like facing my father when I'd done something bad or he thought I had. Entering a kind of mental estivation, I stayed alert – typically the private soldier is incapable of totally ignoring an enigmatic Major sitting five feet from him. Perhaps I thought about the pistol I'd seen downtown and lusted after. Perhaps I pondered the Manzano mountains, low brownish foothills dotted with pale scrubby trees and fluffy brush, visible through the glare beyond a hazy window, a comfortable place to rest my gaze even if I had to keep my head turned to hold the view. What I didn't think about was the absoluteness of the dictatorship I'd entered on enlisting. The feelings were the same, though this officer bore little resemblance to my father. It never entered my mind to ask, "What's this all about?" In the moment, ignorant but not yet afraid, I was years from realizing that this way of "parking" tension amounted to a kind of dreamtime.

The end of the session was as uncanny as the session itself, which had lasted nearly two hours when I saw a clock. The major, for the first time looking directly at me, said,

Oh yes, I need a writing sample from you. Sign your name a couple times on this, and tore off a yellow sheet from his pad. Full of questions, I however said only

OK – uh, sir. I signed my name and looked up. The major said in a flat voice,

Another one, and when I had done it, the major said
That's all.

I sat there a few more seconds, prompting him to say,
You can go.

My head swimming, I left having learned exactly nothing about what had just happened. Anachronously I recalled Bob Manning defending his resistance to Special Weapons school:

I just won't have it, that's all – and I've still got a Congressman. Do you guys? Why that came up I don't know. I was not conscious of being abused.

Sergeant Logan knew absolutely nothing either, or said he didn't, and had nothing to say in support of my feelings, poorly or barely expressed in any case. This baffled private wasn't angry in the least – what to be angry about? But a dark tinge seeped into my being. I couldn't exactly call it "fear," but that's what it was, nameless anxiety. It permeated the subsequent days, a psychic tape-loop. I spoke to no one about it beyond my single confused query of Logan. With no friend to talk with, I was perplexed about the interview, and thought nobody could have helped me with that. Months ago, sitting with a clipboard in a boring basic training lecture, I'd begun to practice signing my name with my right hand, adopting with modification my father's elaborate calligraphic signature. At the end of basic I was issued a permanent ID card, which I signed with my new right-hand signature; but I remained otherwise left-handed in writing. Perched before that major, I scrawled as directed, mind squirming with whether to reveal this quirk of ambidexterity, feeling odd, eccentric. But I kept quiet, wondering if I'd screwed up. Except for that minor "lie," my weird feelings about the interview went away – until the company clerk again told me to report to Building 208 that afternoon. I felt brief panic but dismissed it as irrational. I had done nothing; I was clean.

This time I entered Building 208 in control of myself, self-assured, determined to get to the bottom of this major's peculiar behavior. But Grieden took charge immediately, gave me no opening to ask a question. To boot, smiling slightly, he was almost cordial, which took me by surprise.

So – you're from a large family, I take it.
Yes sir...
Catholic, I suppose?
No, sir – I mean, I was raised Catholic, but it didn't take.

He grinned crookedly, looked me in the eye a long time and said,

What do you call yourself now?
Nothing, sir – *maybe agnostic.* I found myself unable to use the word "atheist" to this man I didn't know. I was not shy about using it in the barracks. The major asked general questions. I talked with difficulty about my youth, my many siblings, avoiding bad stuff like my father's polio, but enthused about hunting and fishing. And no, I didn't have a girlfriend.

Why'd you join the Army?
Instantly wary, I tried to be cagey. My words are gone, but likely I didn't mention the GI Bill. Perhaps I managed some bullshit about service, or seeing the world, maybe even a self-conscious assertion about "duty to one's country." I now felt on dangerous ground without knowing why, and tried fumblingly to set myself on a track of innocence, though I had no cause for guilt. But this officer's intentions were unknown. I noticed

clearly that the stiffness of power barely softened a rasping edge to the man's jocularity.

That's all.

Again I was let go, but informed I was expected back next week, same time. I had no conscious idea that this was a security matter, not even when Logan took me aside and said it would be "a good idea" if I went over to the Motor Pool for a few days and learned how to operate a fork lift. Sarge spoke in his usual confiding way and I perceived nothing out of the ordinary. Quickly energized by the novelty of "heavy equipment," I seconded his "suggestion" immediately. Company A had learned we'd soon have a depot function added to our mission: storing and transporting weapons, as well as our regular test and maintenance work. Developing multiple skills seemed to be in the battalion air and I had no reason to think Sarge was anything but straight with me. Later when it was over Logan confirmed my suspicion. He went into his "older brother" tone, and I realized I had been sequestered from direct weapons work – "temporarily recessed" in his words. Sarge, usually careful with language, had slipped, realized it and tried to cover it:

No, a TDY assignment.

Temporary duty indeed, I thought. I was no fool; until that moment I could trust Sarge. Suddenly I was afraid to speak, to show any hint of anxiety by asking "What's going on?" as if the question itself might somehow send a wrong, possibly dangerous message to Major Grieden. I kept my mouth shut. *TDY, bullshit!*

The sessions with Grieden continued, each bringing a spasm of irrational dread, which heightened into savage self-examination as I searched for any trace remembrance or slip I might have made that could even vaguely be construed as a "security breach." I saw that my self-cudgelling was repeating Catholic confessional behavior of not so many years before. I had long since contemptuously derided the pronouncement by some saint long forgotten, *"Give me a child until he is seven and I will have him for life."* Later, my atheism more articulate, I took pains to acquire the text of the Nicene Creed from a college roommate, a devout Catholic apprenticed to a CIA career. Fending off the guy's curiosity, I read that bedrock doctrine closely, studied it – and consciously disavowed each sentence of it in turn.

Nothing bad had happened to me yet, but I couldn't lay aside feelings of ominous foreboding. Why me? None of the other guys were in this situation. Why was I in this fix – if it was one? Did somebody finger me? On what basis? Perhaps those days had not seen common press usage of the phrase "fishing expedition" in reporting on investigations. I was a Private E-1. I could not read official minds, could not summon the *sang-froid* to stand apart from this absurd entanglement. My thought spiralled into psychic *culs-de-sac*, hurt idealism – yes, that absolutist virtue intrinsic to narcissism. Nothing was happening, I had done nothing; what the hell was going on here? There were no straightforward inquiries from the major, nothing like interrogation. I felt treated as a specimen, as if this major was waiting for me to make a telling move or something. Incapable of candor with anyone of superior rank, under stress I was the same with myself. Habitual introspection, always tending toward the morbid, saw me start to withdraw from social interaction in the barracks. I took refuge in the good-and-evil prose of the shoot-'em-up novels from the day room, reading again what had killed time my first days at Sandia. I tried to watch television, but left the dayroom if guys started asking me questions. At work I quickly attained modest proficiency running a huge forklift under the tutelage of Chavez, battalion motor sergeant, a rough-talking but benign Apache from Oklahoma. The work absorbed me and kept my mind off the unreality of this off-the-wall major. Unconsciousness of the passage of time, occupied mind and body with physical work, I sought my bunk early, got up very early for a hearty and leisurely breakfast with the ever good-natured cooks.

I started each day consciously preparing for whatever might come.

The meaning behind the interviews emerged without warning. Grieden suddenly asked me if I had ever used such-and-such a dry cleaning service downtown. Surprised, I answered in the negative. I had to do so several times on repeated questioning and finally I said I owned no clothes which needed dry cleaning, thinking that the admission made me look weird. But it seemed to satisfy the major, though it didn't show on his face. Silence. Feeling released by this first substantive question after all these weeks, I spoke up as if a weight had lifted,
Why do you ask?

The major showed a flash of annoyance at the question and ignored it to ask his own:
Do you take notes in the training classes?

Immediately rebuffed, I felt gooseflesh start. I remembered my handwriting "lie of omission." I wondered whether to now reveal that ambidexterous filip and the grilling it might provoke. I decided to say nothing, managed to somehow hide a momentary chill and answered him,
No, sir – they said not too, that we wouldn't need them.
You never write down stuff and take it with you?
Yes sir – I mean no, sir; I mean, I don't take notes at all.
Are you sure?
Yes sir.
Are you very sure?
Yes sir.

But in fact there had been a friendly argument with a barracks-mate at the beer hall after payday, weeks ago, beer and chips flowing freely, in which to prove a point I'd made a crude sketch of the Mark 6 warhead on a napkin. But I distinctly remembered tearing it into small bits afterward, nervous at the time about breaking security off-duty. As these things go, remembering this technical lie may have passed across my face, for the major repeated,

Ever?

Yes, sir. I met and held his eyes. He stared at me it seemed a full minute, then said,

You can go.

Now that I knew something about the major's game, fear came to the fore. Am I some kind of suspect? Why again did I not ask my interrogator? His rebuff to my attempt to do so intimidated me, deepened my helplessness. I felt trapped and hunted, not at all reassured by the concrete if sketchy facts that had emerged. I was caught. Perhaps as well my failure to rise above fear lay in awareness of scapegoat behavior perhaps waiting grimly – an image came, of a snapping turtle in dark water – in the underbelly of the military, the mother of all authoritarian hierarchies. Paralyzed; there was nothing I could do. Basically obedient, I felt no open anger then. I swallowed the episode like a bitter pill. Acceptance had to be my lot. I had volunteered for this, it was a normal part of military life, get used to it. So much for being a fucking "élite" soldier. Grimly I thought of Manning and Branch, how spooked they had been.

Espionage was rife in those cloak-and-dagger days of the Red scare. Spies and double agents were everywhere, from every country, involved in fierce national and international intrigue about what really went on in Sandia Base and up at Los Alamos. I had no clue back then – who did? – about the hermetic necrosis of military secrecy, the black infrastructure of nuclear superiority, had no clue to what comprised information useful to its deadly serious purpose. I had no inkling that Grieden's interviews were evaluations of my "psychological stability," or that I had passed scrutiny. For a long time I thought that this Major was simply some kind of "sniffer" somehow keyed on me as a subject to be "checked out."

Nothing Grieden ever said betrayed human warmth toward me. I followed Army rules, mostly, did in fact keep my nose clean, self-protectively but also from deeply reflexive obedience made automatic in early life. In the end I got nothing from this hardass officer even during what proved to be the last session, when Grieden spoke of "pieces of paper" with "sketches" and "sensitive information" on them which had turned up in an Albuquerque dry cleaning shop and were somehow retrieved by an FBI agent.

I don't suppose you know anything about that.

No, sir.

Then as usual, Grieden, staring at me without expression, said,

You can go.

Logan said,

There's more FBI agents in Albuquerque than any city in the whole country.

Not long after my ordeal, a post-level security scandal hit the Albuquerque newspaper. A guard permitted to pass through the gate a lieutenant whose badge photo was actually a mug shot of a black bear. What happened to the unfortunate MP who failed to compare face to photo is not recorded but, newly restored to my crew, I joined in the sarcastic coffee-break jeers.

This dumb fuckin Army – thinking they could catch a spy with silly shit like that. But my own laughter was sour, and only half-heartedly did I second the cynical whooping of the guys, which toned down abruptly when Warrant Officer Ford came along. Nobody spoke up for the scapegoat MP, simply because he was an MP. So far as I knew, I was the only man in the 14th to undergo security scrutiny, if that's what it was. Others may have been, probably had, but I never heard anything more. Like me, those guys no doubt avoided recounting what they went through. By the end of that anxiety-mill I was in a bad place, again feeling the radiation of the old inner "glowing coal" from high school days, feeling no anger, but consciously girding myself for anything dangerous that might come without notice. With no psychology vocabulary, I conceived this "glowing coal" only as "will" and could not recognize it as generalized fear because it was non-specific; it was a seed of paranoia corrosive of self-respect long malnourished. Unable to stand aside and perceive my posture as extreme defensiveness, what stood in was a grim non-verbal attitude of *never say die*, masquerading alternately as steely determination to "get ahead," or passionate desire to be elsewhere. If I just hung on long enough it would make me tough. Thus, tacit acceptance of the dehumanizing militarist doctrine and my own inability to see myself mirroring it. Years later, approaching an acute threshold in my worsening condition, I was electrified by Dee Brown's story of Crazy Horse coming to his penultimate moment of truth. I believed I knew those awful feelings, felt myself inside that Lakota head, as if I were Crazy Horse myself at his stunning realization of imminent imprisonment when, struggling to wrench free of Little Big Man's grasp he was bayoneted by the other guard.

The same thing could happen to me at any time, to any of us. That harsh and nebulous resolve was mixed of current oppression and reinforced by pre-military family conditioning, therefore mine to dissolve. How ridiculous it seems, but in the moment I made a vow: they would find me ready when they came for me. I was coping as best I could, controlling anonymous demons that could destroy me if I wasn't ready. Certain imponderables were beyond my unschooled mind. McCarthy's "Red menace" hearings had by then given a terrorist aura to the label "security risk"; and the nuclear enterprise had incorporated psychology into its personnel evaluations. My excesses of rage, more inner than outer, made me sometimes think I was "crazy." I dwelt morbidly on my Mom's brother and his son, both of them institutionalized for decades at Staunton.

These reactive ruminations about Major Grieden gradually waned and found relief in a new pistol I had seen downtown and whose acquisition was but a matter of time. Battalion regulations allowed personal firearms, but they were to be stored with the quartermaster. Later, having bought the sixshooter, I told no one and dismissed thought of obediently giving it up to the supply sergeant. Sergeant Kayo had said our personal weapons would be readily available; but Kayo was not around weekends and I wanted it to be *always* available. It was a .22, a toy, though that word didn't occur to me then. Dangerous, of course but essentially a plaything. I'd never in my life known homicidal rage. By keeping the piece in my footlocker, padlocked, I was merely asserting a quasi-military prerogative. As an élite soldier I was confident that battalion informality would preclude disciplinary action if my transgression came to light. If I did land in hot water, I was ready to argue ignorance or lack of intent, ready to put on careful "injured innocence."

I was a doer, not a thinker, almost always ready to drop serious stuff and go drink beer with the guys, or read a book or see a movie. Or uncover the new sixshooter if no one was around, just to handle it, admire the glovelike fit of the handmade holster, enjoy the solid reality of the ensemble, black steel and warm brown leather. However there seemed no way to achieve using it. Sandia Base was urban and I had no car. But I was perfectly patient with my secret. Having no buddy I could or would trust, I kept the revolver to myself. I found myself gazing often at distant Sandia peak, incipient dreamtime, ignoring the cluster of communication towers on the summit, enrapt in the green mystery of the ponderosa pine forest behind the rugged scarp. How big was it? How wild? Was it watered?

X
ORI

At work the game notched up in seriousness. One morning we wheeled into the bay a caisson unlike any seen before, but obviously a Mark 6. Perhaps its subtle strangeness lay in the yellow data-legend stencilled on new OD paint, or perhaps in the official lead wire seal on the right rear corner bolt; maybe both together. Mr. Yardley circled around it silently, all business, which got our full attention. Something portentous and not a little exciting had come our way.

This is a live one, men, said Yardley. Eight ears perked up; everything to date had been dummy warheads. We waited alertly as our chief studied the numbers and made notes on his clipboard.

I said aloud, *A live warhead this close to downtown?*

Don't worry 'bout that, men, said Yardley, *we won't even see the cone assembly. No danger at all,* he said – as if a stupendous explosive detonation scattering plutonium far and wide was nothing to worry about.

Shortly we got into it, working with subdued concentration and renewed consultation of the Top Secret manual. It was our first live weapon off the line, or so he said. If Yardley said it was a live weapon we had to believe him. The differences between a practice device and one "off the line" were subtle. I'd long noticed that some warheads showed signs of being "shopworn," with lengthy histories recorded on their inspection log cards.

How could one tell? Perhaps the difference was encoded in the stencilled number-letter codes we had not the key to. We never saw any cone assemblies, essential for nuclear detonation. Perhaps even Mr. Yardley didn't really know whether a given bomb was live or a dummy. Where did these devices come from? Where did they go after maintenance and testing and re-sealing? These were questions with no answers, queries I had to learn not to ask because the guys looked at me funny if I did.

Mr. Yardley, supervising, suddenly seemed to have difficulty keeping his hands off this live warhead on its workstand. Inserting himself into our process, seeming nervous but trying to dissemble, but clumsily, he passed his unease to us by contagion. We took his intrusiveness to mean we weren't being careful enough or precise enough, or didn't know the protocol we'd practiced for weeks. As we worked tension built until man-mountain Moose said with a little half-scowling chuckle,

Wa-il, boys, should we hang 'im by his belt from the chain hoist and get him outta our damn way? That broke the tension and we all laughed, even Yardley, still ill at ease with his new status as a Warrant Officer. A short time earlier he'd been a master sergeant, career enlisted, was therefore not without leadership and command experience. But now he was a hybrid, in between, with both privilege and responsibility but without the pay – or promotion potential – of a commissioned officer.

Okay okay – you're right men, I'll just stand back and watch – that's what I'm s'posed to do anyway.

How many live ones came through our bays? Many; by then we'd been told that the HE of this bomb was difficult to detonate accidentally; improvements in the stuff had nearly eliminated that danger without compromising its explosive power. We worked deliberately, studiously, feeling we were doing what was called for with high skill and competence.

On a Friday afternoon, word went round of a company party, free beer in the dayroom after work, everybody invited. Maybe even the CO would be there. But no officers showed up to gather round the keg, installed in an ice filled garbage can, only sergeants sitting beside us privates, everybody buddy-buddy, much coarse and jolly old-soldier talk, no food, beer and war stories, and after awhile some of us were getting tipsy. The keg was big enough to wipe out A Company even had everybody shown up. A joke was made that it was our duty to finish it off: if the damn Army was generous enough to provide it, that made it G.I. beer, Government Issue, meant to be consumed like ammo or C-rations – like ourselves for that matter – and the Army didn't want to see it again.

In time, the non-coms made tactical departures, went home to wives and families before anybody was out-and-out drunk. Guys went off to the mess hall, ate and returned to work on the keg some more. Logan, who left early, said there would be more parties like this.

At work seriousness continued to ratchet up. Mr. Yardley started keeping track how long it took his crew to do their work, making notes in a little book. This alarmed us, made us wonder if we'd somehow been "bad boys." He told us to calm down, just do our job at the usual pace so he could time the process for one weapon, complete with its cone assembly. Somebody asked why the record-keeping. Yardley shrugged, spoke vaguely of "Army boiler-plate," which of course it was, important matter-of-fact data, the bottom line in Bertrand Russell's definition of war: *"Maximum slaughter at minimum expense."* None of us had any idea of Bertrand Russell in 1953.

Building a battalion is team-forming. It must have been a heady time for battalion brass and everyone in the know during the escalating Cold War insanity. But we were well-insulated from that. GIs are wrapped in, and wrap themselves in, psychosocial cocoons. To a dogface soldier change happens willy-nilly, with minimal information. Privates are the most malleable clay in the "Table of Organization and Equipment" – the "TO&E" – the official document listing every thing organic and inorganic subsumed under each battalion, each company, platoon, squad and soldier and his uniform. Crew members began to be swapped around for obscure reasons, sometimes temporarily. I was placed in various slots over some weeks; jeep driver, forklift operator, supply handler, donkey labor for the Supply sergeant. Logan went along with Headquarters' wishes but told me not to worry, he wanted and would get me on his crew in the end. No one spoke about interpersonal conflict beginning to manifest in A Company. Battalion HQ wended on in apparent serenity, accreting its official and classified history. The personnel adjustments were mostly expedient, seldom formalized with orders. I stayed under Yardley and Logan, both of whom I "liked."

But I turned stiffly formal when Yardley asked what I thought of this man or that. At those moments the gulf between officer and enlisted gaped wide; I'd die before I'd badmouth a bunkmate, saying I could get along with anybody, pure bullshit, a smooth evasion. No way could I have worked alongside Private Barry, whom I regarded as dangerous since an episode when, verbally teased while trying to nap away a Sunday afternoon, Barry had suddenly whirled up enraged, whipped a pistol from under his pillow and screamed at his tormentors to let him alone or they'd be sorry. It was a tense moment, but the guys backed off and the drama passed. The incident was not reported or otherwise dealt with, no peacemaker arising. I was afraid it would be reported and that a surprise inspection would follow and discover *my* sixshooter. But molasseslike loyalty against the brass prevailed. But Barry's histrionic threat made everybody back off, though the incident sealed his fate as an oddball and he ultimately became a scapegoat.

Yardley tried unsuccessfully to pierce my hedging remarks about my mates. Appealing variously to my intelligence or his own lengthy familiarity with barracks life, he said he knew some in the company rubbed others the wrong way. It was true of course, and once or twice I came close to yielding to his pressure for candor. I was glad Barry's name never came up, and in the end I held to silent – but impure – fealty to the guys I ate and slept and drank beer with. I felt no guilt. Yardley had crossed a line as Warrant Officer, had therefore to be treated with great caution.

We seldom see ourselves as others see us, even more true for me locked up in myself with no detached awareness of the effect of my personality on others. At times I was a good bullshitter. Drinking beer and running my mouth, I might brag about some boyhood hunting exploit or an encounter with a copperhead or a skunk, maybe tell about a "famous" drunk I'd been on, but I tended to push the chatter in a serious direction. I remember making a rant against the obscene wealth of the Vatican in a miserable fucking world. I saw how my tirade put off some guys, and of course I totally missed the irony of the billion-dollar war game *we* were playing. In some moments, I could see myself projecting what I'd call charisma in somebody else, like old Thornberry. This episodic intensity, this "motor-mouthing" blinded me to fact. When this guy or that seemed to want a closer attachment than noisy beer-drinking or a poker game allowed, especially when questioned about "home," I was suddenly intensely shy, might deflect questioning with a monologue, unable to respond authentically. Shifting mental gears, I turtled up in midstream, invisibly I thought. I could smoothly turn aside a transparent compliment with mild self-deprecation, unable to go near some indefinable threat I could only half-recognize, couldn't acknowledge, sensing something shadowy, not terror exactly, a feeling I semi-articulated as some unspecifiable "information," or nonverbal "knowledge," that I would decide was "diagnostic" which became a "sadness" that this particular guy who wanted to be my friend *could* not, maybe even *would* not "understand" me, and had nothing for me in any case. Thus adroitly I projected my deficiency onto the guy, or if that one persisted, I referred my inability to relate to a trivial external circumstance like *I gotta go get my laundry*. Nobody knew me, nobody could know me really, could know what it was like, this something I couldn't have talked about with anyone. The often easy – sometimes I thought "humane" – way I rebuffed a guy only looking for a buddy at times only strengthened that one's efforts to get closer to me, made him try harder, and then I'd strive for a remark soft but unmistakable, perhaps brutal if need be – and that would be the end of it. Inherent in the tale is that much data are gone, not merely repressed, simply unregistered in the moment, my stiff self-absorption blocking incoming perception. Thus the task is reconstructive, without ready access to many compelling, relevant or revealing facts, and only pieces of a picture can form out of too few cogent stories. Judgment as 'choice among options', rather than "worthiness" – is the guideline here, for all along the tortured way I have striven to present accurately the etiology of a case – among other things.

Official adventure supervened: we drove trucks to Shreveport, Louisiana. Sergeant Chavez led the convoy, following us in his huge tank mover. Chavez had warned us it would be a hard trip – *Texas is big – and dry*, he said, winking slyly; our Motor Sergeant was no teetotaler.

The trucks we ferried were decrepit blue Air Farce vehicles. Chavez didn't call them junkers, but that's what he meant, but said not to worry, we'd make it there and come back in Army vehicles in better shape.

Texas *was* big and dry, immense in those days before Interstate Highways, hour on hour of endless treeless scrub. Chavez followed in his wrecker, roaring ahead periodically to points where the route changed. We would camp out halfway there; we had sleeping bags and C-rations. Corporal Shiflett was driving a six-by full of jerry cans of fuel and towing a water trailer. It was bright, windy and cold. We droned on at 50 miles an hour, the road string-straight. Highway-hypnosis became a problem, and in mid-afternoon, the truck ahead of me suddenly swooped into the broad drainage swale, raising a huge cloud of dust.

No damage. It was Private Barry, who swore dully in the face of Chavez's wrath that he had not gone to sleep at the wheel. Nobody believed Private Barry, but we all welcomed the chance to get out and walk around in the cold wind, stretch and breathe and gabble about "this miserable fuckin Texas."

An hour later, the same thing happened to me. All at once I was in the broad swale rolling to a stop in a mixture of weird confusion and huge embarassment. I sat there until suddenly Chavez was yelling something I couldn't hear through the window. I turned off the engine and opened the door. The endless Plains wind tried to wrench it from my grasp – and released fumes from the cab to Chavez's nose.

Aha! he shouted, *these goddam ol' clunkers! Carbon monoxide! You coulda killed yourself! You okay? Can you still drive? You don' hafta, you can change off.*

With who? I thought; we had no spare drivers. I said,

I'm alright. I had to repeat it several times to satisfy his gruff solicitude.

Chavez waved everybody around, then said,

From now on I don wanna see no closed windows! Carbon monoxide kills ya without you knowin it! You got field jackets, it ain't that cold, and I don wanna see nobody else run off the goddam road. Maybe you think I'm pushin you – I am, but that's so we have slack on the way back – have some fun. I got a nice surprise waitin for us. He winked as he had before.

You keep those windows cracked, ya hear? Mount up!

At full dark we wheeled into a barren roadside park, circled and stopped nose to tail like frontier wagons. A short distance away were lights, a town. Beer was quickly on my mind. Chavez disappeared after changing into cowboy boots, a black ten-gallon hat and a gorgeous snap shirt that I thought of as "brocade." Shiflett said Chavez had family up the road and wouldn't be back till morning. Somebody suggested we check out the town. We could get away with fatigues in this one-horse outback, and soon I was walking toward the lights with my crewmate Red.

Muleshoe, Texas: one restaurant still open, about to close,

Sorry, no beer sold in this county. We stood disappointed under the greenish fluorescent glare, dry-mouthed and red-eyed, bitching in low voices so the stout country girl behind the counter wouldn't hear us.

That damn Chavez! What a godforsaken place he put us in! He did it for a reason, keep us out of trouble...

The sole option for something to drink was buttermilk. Red, upbeat and cheerful, was a Minnesota beer-lover, yet here he was praising dairy products, buttermilk in particular, urging me to try it – damn, no beer! We ended up buying a cold quart each and sat on the curb outside talking and drinking the stuff, thick and rich like a sour milkshake. Good, but not beer. In a few words we disposed of this two-bit, rolled-up Texas backwater. Red was strongly against the death penalty. We didn't talk about whatever the Rosenbergs had done or not done, we couldn't have possibly followed the case, but agreed that hanging them was wrong. We finished the buttermilk and sauntered without talk back to the park. We made Barksdale AFB the next day, got Army trucks, few enough that we could take turns driving and riding back.

The Army vehicles had no sissy governors on their strong engines and I rode the whole way "home" in a tractor trailer, Melton claiming he was happy to drive. That was a trial for me, and after awhile I argued unsuccessfully for a change-off. He established that I didn't know what "double-clutching" was, that you had to know that in order to drive this beast. In late afternoon, leaving behind country of walking-beam oil pumps – I thought of prehistoric monsters – Chavez suddenly took the lead and shortly we turned north. Sandia was west, not north. What was going on? We halted and gathered. Chavez said that a few minutes away was a roadhouse with the best damn catfish and hush-puppies in all Oklahoma. When he said "Oklahoma" cheers went up: beer! As for me, I was instantly hungry at the prospect of catfish. Virginia culture, deeper south than the deep south, was not deep-south enough to have taught me what in hell a "hush-puppy" was. But catfish and beer, too! This Chavez was alright!

We shortly descended into a broad, gentle valley, crossed the Red River and stopped in a line along the road across from a big sign: *Catfish & Hushpuppies – All you can eat $1*. This was Chavez's home country, Melton said,

He knows it like the back of his hand. We left the teetotalers to eat their C-rations by themselves, walked across a gravelly parking lot and up two steps into a big low-ceilinged tavern with a long bar facing the entrance. A beautiful fresh-faced girl with high breasts stared at us, her red mouth wide open at so many GIs trooping in without notice. She stopped what she was doing at the counter and disappeared, forever. Almost as many other men sat around the place as GIs. I noticed hard stares from these locals and said,

Don't seem like we're very welcome here.

Melton, from Arkansas, smiled broadly and said,
Oh yeah we are, alright... And then,
Good – we'll have a couple beers, some catfish, then probably have some fun.

After long silence punctuated by a twanging juke box, a burly sorrowful-looking man emerged from somewhere, began taking orders, bringing bottles of beer, saying,

The catfish ain't quite ready – wasn't expecting this many people – but it'll be good when it comes, don' worry bout that, an' plenty of it.

Sitting together, slaking our thirst, bathed in the mournful self-abnegation of shit-kicker music, dodging slashing sundown light, listening to Chavez brag on *Red River catfish, the best in the country*, we began to unwind from driving, no thought where we'd sleep tonight – probably the back of a six-by with no air mattress. Lost is how many rounds we drank. No fish appeared. Hungry GIs began to grumble. The bartender tried to placate us, saying,

When it gits here, it'll be plumb fresh – hell, some of 'em are still swimmin'. Don' worry, they'll be here soon.

Suddenly came huge steaming platters of golden-brown hush puppies and plates loaded with fragrant white-meat catfish – "Channel cats, caught today." With coleslaw and bottles of ketchup and more beer and laughter, everybody pigged out, especially me, going back more than once, for thirds maybe fourth helpings – *All you can eat for a dollar!* We were flying high and whooping it up, but I noticed that the hard stares of the locals were being reciprocated, which made me uneasy.

Yeah, said Melton, smirking grimly, *mebbe we gonna have fun soon.*

More people arrived as the night deepened. Soon it was shoulder to shoulder in the crowded joint, all guys, busy eating and drinking and laughing, the juke box jangling, and I happened to be looking in the right direction when a local launched a big hard fist straight across a table into Red's face. All hell broke loose as if on cue, probably the case. The next moment Chavez was swinging a chair over his head. It landed on a table scattering beer bottles but missing its intended target, who got his own chair into action as *Pan Demonium* came in and sat down for a spell to watch men bash one another to the clatter of bottles breaking and crashing, beer sloshing everywhere now, and then a fist went by my face as I sat near stupefaction by the warm glow of catfish and beer in my belly. The punch-thrower, drunk, had simply missed me. I'd done nothing to merit this, but the near-miss galvanized me, jerked me to my feet on the slippery floor.

This sure as hell is none of my business! Bent over and keeping low, I sighted the door through the uproarious jangling ballet and snaked through wooden and fleshy legs like a bittern slips through cattails. I escaped the punch-up clean and untouched to stand tipsy in the cool dark night listening with fearful amazement as the fighting roared on, wondering tipsily if I should be "doing something," not knowing what that would be; and after a while people started backing out the door fighting, and then here came Red out of the dark, swearing,

That sonofabitch got as good as he gave me, by God, grinning crookedly, holding a bloody handkerchief to his nose. Then Melton came out, still swinging at a guy who would not leave the safety of the building for the dark outside, Melton yelling hoarsely,

S'matter wit' you? No more fun? I thought you assholes liked fun.

A couple guys came out, arms locked around each other, stumbled and fell down the steps into the crunchy gravel, their impact breaking them apart to let them pummel each other some more, the banging and roaring continuing inside even after all of us had cleared out:

They're fighting each other now! Why? What the hell's going on here? Then Chavez burst out the door roaring like a bear.

Sonsabitches! Sonsabitches! I'll show 'em, lousy bastards, fuck wi' me you fuck wi' the bull! He stomped down the steps and headed across the highway for his huge beloved tank-retriever. Shiflett yelled from the dark,

Stop him! The crazy bastard's gonna drive the wrecker into the place!

But nobody went after this wild Apache, untouchable because he was a Master Sergeant, whom later I imagined came from the fierce Mescalero survivors of Bosque Redondo – though I knew nothing about that genocidal event then. Chavez actually got the engine started, managed to get the huge machine into gear and turned halfway onto the highway, aiming it at the flimsy building before his corporal, yelling and trying to calm his boss, finally got into the cab and turned off the ignition, took the key. Chavez bellowed at his assistant's "treason," promised to "court martial" him for "insubordination." Shiflett, winking at us, just grinned at his boss.

The next morning, late, the sun already up, guys washing up at the water mule, pissing by truck fenders, the roadhouse deserted and forlorn in its own big hangover, Chavez came along the line softly, in beaded moccasins, slit-eyed and seeking eye contact with us, his smile tightened by a split lip and muttering,

How'd ya like them catfish?

Perhaps it didn't happen exactly that way, though it could have, probably it did from some slightly different curlicue of memory. Beyond my hangover – not that bad – curled up on a hard bench in Melton's cab, or maybe in the curtained back of a six-by, desiccated and thirsty, I was in a definite "altered state," as if I was outside myself, gone somewhere, completely lost and floating but totally conscious, able to survey my discöordination from afar, seeing myself a speck of cosmic dust in an infinite universe unfathomable but not evil, one totally unknowable, vast, incomprehensible. And this was only a dream, not a seed needing nurture or anything, and then somewhere in my being, in the plicated complexity of all the stuffed pain of my life came a vague and fugitive feeling that it was all right, definitely OK, to leave behind such foolish shit as this. Daydreaming and drinking water, nodding off to be jerked awake again by an ill pitch of road or pothole, I thought,

What the hell am I doing here?

XI
Kill

Alright, men, said Yardley, interrupting coffee chatter, *break's over – this is now a meeting. Refill your cup if you want to, but stick around.*

When we had settled he said,
What we got is an ORI coming up.
What's ORI?
Operational Readiness Inspection. They're gonna send inspectors – officers – to watch us to see if we're up to snuff. It'll be a complete live weapons drill, including cone assembly.

We had been working toward the ORI without knowing it. The training protocol had for months included a final test culminating in simulated nuclear arming, at times with a dummy cone assembly. But we'd never gone the whole route with actual plutonium. Thus we listened raptly to Yardley: in this official, probably chickenshit, ORI, we would work on a live warhead from a line depot, perform the complete protocol – SOP – with inspectors watching over our shoulders.

We were a little scared – some admitting it only to themselves. Silent for a day, we displaced our anxiety by querying Yardley about "hazardous duty pay." This was the big leagues, the real thing, dangerous, and we ought to get paid extra for it, like jump pay for paratroopers, never mind that paratroopers packed their own chutes. Yardley went away, to talk to Captain Turner it turned out, came back in few minutes and said,

No way, men. Nobody's ever been killed doing this job, so no hazardous duty pay, and that's it.

We grumbled a while, but we ate it. Of course we knew nothing about the people and sheep getting sick and dying of radiation poisoning up in Utah. Yardley knew no more than we did about the details of the impending inspection. At least it wouldn't happen immediately. Would it take place here?

You bet.

Live weapons right next to downtown Albuquerque? I asked the question silently this time. It seemed not a question to anyone else. Things got moving; in the work bays and off duty we young and not-so-young warriors began to move with new gravity. We were approaching the threshold of professionalism, and for a time the coming test seemed to flesh out our tenuous notions of ourselves as "élite" soldiers, though we would have laughed at the notion coming from an officer; we knew full well we were just GIs.

Another Friday afternoon beer party was announced. The brass was clearly following a protocol: morale-building. This time the battalion CO would be on hand, a mysterious colonel known to be a Catholic, said even to attend Mass regularly, a brilliant mind who had been deeply involved in the fiasco of that gigantic howitzer designed to throw a 280mm nuclear shell at the Russians from western Europe. With a barrel appropriate to a naval cruiser, if not the Big Mo itself, it could fling nuclear rounds over the horizon with deadly accuracy. The only trouble was, the damned thing was supposed to be mobile artillery, moved by monster rubber-tired tractors fore and aft like a hook-and-ladder. It sucked up four gallons of fuel per mile. Slow and ungainly, it was thus a perfect target for return fire. Perforce it was limited to the famous Autobahn. Few European country roads could accommodate its gargantuan bulk, and off-road it sank into sitting-duck immobility.

All the same, the colonel's involvement – the Exec Officer's term – gave added cachet to our commander's rank, even if he wasn't a bird colonel. Or so it appeared to me, ever attentive to bits of intelligence about the brass. Other officers spoke in reserved, even hushed tones about this famous Colonel Healy, a soft-spoken man, fit but slightly pudgy, always in impeccable dress uniform, genial, frequently away from Sandia, said to be at the Pentagon "on business." Most of us enlisted men had only ever seen him; few had spoken with him. Soon he would be making the rounds of the bays, it was said. With the ORI coming up, he wanted to observe his men, make contact with us.

Relax, Sarge said, *don't be afraid of him, do your work same as always and if he shows up at your elbow on the job don't bother to salute, just be yourself.*

I was instantly put off on hearing about the CO's Catholicism. Moral anxiety rose up, inducing tension I could not have spoken about, even tipsy. This self-argument, ever ready to spring, dated from that senior year encounter with Sister Joseph. Underlying everything we were taught in Religion class, always, was Free Will, she had said, a "lesson" I seized as fervently as simplistically: reactive mental refuge from paternal and churchly oppression. If a person committed a "mortal" sin, so-called in that special lingo where actual lethality was irrelevant, and did so knowingly, and if that person was ready to take the consequences, then so be it – 'Free Will' was everything. To a tormented teenager the rationalist fantasy, closely, deeply and privately held, was worth the risk. Eternal damnation? Hah!

But now I found myself worrying how I might be questioned, for the CO was said to have taken a personal hand in picking his battalion from holding company drones and was said to be "quite familiar" with what amounted to our resumés – mine would have filled half a page at most. In my morose ruminations this unknown colonel seemed to combine and embody, if hazily, ecclesiastic and military power in one skin. He was therefore somebody to stay the hell away from.

In the shuffling around of men among the crews, it came to pass that Moose Myrick would be a permanent member of our crew. A big Kansan, Moose was rumored to be recently out of the brig, busted from Sergeant to Pfc because of a binge that ended in broken-head fighting. He'd seen a tour in Korea and was the largest male specimen I'd ever been around. He towered over me, just under seven feet tall, 350 pounds, possessed of enormous strength. Yet in his first days with us a cheerful, tentative, bashful quality, almost childlike, characterized him. He was strangely obsequious, mystifying me until at coffee he openly expressed contrition for some crime unspecified, saying how glad he was to escape a Dishonorable Discharge and to have gotten this second chance. Responding to his effusive *mea culpa* coming out of the blue, I said merely,

It's OK, Moose – we've all fucked up one time or another. Later I wondered if his breast-beating meant this was more than a second chance, maybe even a *last* chance.

But it's not my responsibility to lay out the character of Moose. Even less justifiably could I scapegoat him. We stayed on the same crew for the rest of my enlistment, which meant we reached at least minimal compatibility in working together. Look at it: by and large we were typical American males, well acculturated, learned and practiced in traditional male rôles, conditioned and protected by effective social armor against living as free men in open, supportive relations with each other and our world. Thus we postured ritually as much as related to one another, spoke of each other as "good ole boys" when fitting, with all the rote warmth implied in that hackneyed and indefinable phrase. Essentially we remained strangers while our practiced hands fondled nuclear hideousness.

The circle gathered around the keg in the dayroom centered of course on the colonel, everyone attentive to him with one ear cocked while seeming to converse with a seatmate – the officers, that is. Sergeants and corporals sat largely mute, and the shy privates, invited to sit, mostly stood, our backs to the yellow cinderblock walls. Late afternoon sun blasted zig-zag stripes across one and all until Logan rose and turned the venetian blind slats to, unblinding more than one of us.

The colonel sipped one paper cup of beer, slowly, speaking in a soft voice with those near him, and soon departed, smiling genially at us. Then the Exec Officer left, and the lieutenants, and the Battalion Top Sergeant, who said he had to go or pay the price with his wife, of whose wrath he claimed to be terrified. His exit was hailed with general whooping jeers; and then we settled to our task. At first it was jovial release, the end of the work week, the old soldiers dominating with war stories from WW2, much guffawing survivor laughter, us green privates listening to how we never had it so good, me mostly taking it in, soon feeling "out of it" but gamely trying to enter the camaraderie. Battle tales eventually gave way to remniscences of bad food and good wine, salted with crude remarks about foreign women. References to combat death emerged piecemeal in a sort of code: stern looks, head shakes, sober pauses without detail. Intently I watched, fascinated at this "pulling rank" on us greenhorns. And soon enough I was affected by a dark chill seeping through the jovial displays of pecking order: the alien and unknowable difference separating men who have killed from those who haven't.

Eventually guys drifted off to chow. I moved closer to the keg, sat beside Logan. Beer was flowing freely now, and I was doing my part. The colonel's low-key participation had freed inhibitions. Soon I was guiltlessly tipsy, trying vainly to follow stories others had perhaps heard before, rendering them disjointed to me. I found meager gratification in this or that specimen of barracks language. Most of my speech answered smiling sarcasm or taunting questions from the old-timers. I enjoyed parrying their verbal jabs, twisting them back onto the asker, occasionally winning an indulgent nod from a non-com with my smiling defiant retort. General steam-letting it was, increasingly noisy, not centered on me, at times unintelligible, which led me into interior conversation – these guys were a garrulous lot.

Moose, as if waiting his turn, the WWII stories having tailed off, began to ramble about Korea. Rising din made it hard for me to understand him. Quiet and lightheaded, I came to when Logan addressed me.

No, I told him, *I'm not feeling bad, I'm feeling good, just that I can't understand much of what's going on, I'm too young to know much anyway.*

Logan said,

Z'alright, it's just bullshit, don' mean nothin. He continued in his uncle voice, something about how when he'd made Sergeant in Germany he'd *bought an electric razor* – me now listening attentively to Moose go on about frontline duty in Korea *and kept it in the car* stuff about trenches and bunkers *got a cigar lighter adaptor* going weeks without a hot meal *meant I didn' have to go home if we had evening inspection* grubby and stinking and colder'n a witch's teat, how the truce basically meant women and showers and a proper bunk in rear "etchelon," how they continued to go out to the front line every morning in sixbys *I'm one of those with a blue beard, you see* just like going to a job, back to barracks at night, how every morning they'd see some gook farmer going off *It grows too fast for one shave a day* with his honeybucket on his head – fertilizer for the fields – and how one morn- *You'll learn tricks like that, too – if you live long enough* somebody took a shot at him and missed, made him run, Moose into it now, obviously high, everybody listening and smiling, making him repeat stuff when he slurred, Moose saying how you couldn't resist a running target, how they cheered when a round broke the big crock of shit and drenched the farmer, who would whirl around and shake his fists at them, dancing with rage – *jes hoppin he was so mad* – and how after awhile it got to be a gook'd start running soon as he saw a six-by coming, Moose acting it out with a kind of terrible artlessness, with Kansas country-boy story-teller authenticity, just having a *good ole time* at this buddy-buddy battalion get-together...

And how sometimes the shot was low and hit the farmer,
But it din matter, haill, there'd be another'n the next mornin'.

To my eternal credit I responded from authentic values, but after that, cosmic inevitability ruled.

What I remember is the speed of that massive arm coming at me roundhouse like an oar, Moose's red eyes dull with the first and only lethal hatred I have ever encountered, everything in slow motion, my hands starting to go up, at the last moment jumping to my feet with speed I would have thought impossible drunk. The stone fist aimed at my head took me instead in the ribs, bowled me aside, clattering my chair. I reeled backward into the cinderblocks, striking my head but feeling no pain and sank to the linoleum. Men instantly piled on Moose who was roaring and bellowing,
Lemme at 'im – I'm gonna kill that pigfuckin' son of a bitch!

On the floor, I didn't lose consciousness. Getting up wobbly in the uproar, Logan at my side calmly told me I'd better leave, they'd take care of Moose, go on to barracks, Moose roaring and bellowing but starting to run down, struggling with his captors, sliding hoarsely into what I heard as self-pity and lamentation, even sobbing, and the last thing this smart-ass lawgiving private heard as I went out the dayroom door was old Corporal Casey yelling at Moose,
Let him go, Moose, he's just a fuckin' kid, a goddam know-it-all, couldn pour piss out of a boot. FUCK HIM! It ain' worth it, Moose.

Thus my stiffest encounter with moral rigidity entirely my own. Fierce anger had just grabbed me and broken open at Moose's punch line.

Moose! The man-mountain had turned when I yelled. He was wiping his mouth with his hand.

That was murder, Moose. Logan instantly elbowed me in the ribs, but I was focussed, ignoring the hubbub, Logan vainly yanking my sleeve. The great round back wrenched around squarely, Moose squinting, head down in feral suspicion,

Whut?

Our eyes locked.

I said, *That was murder.* So I'd asked for it plain and simple, thrown a square challenge at a man known as a hot-tempered brawler.

I couldn't let it pass, I told Logan later.

Well, why not something less provocative? Like "Aw, you're just bullshittin us, Moose."

Later, alone, self-pityingly 'processing the incident', I saw how incorrect were my assumptions about this ignorant lout. I wasn't trying to "lord it over" a reformed and penitent newcomer. Moose outranked me with years of service seniority, all-important in the Army. But only much later I saw how moral superiority had taken hold of me since the big man's confession that first morning on our crew. With conceit I thought concealed, I savored, even felt proud remembering my poised attention during the buildup of Moose's tale, sitting expectantly, almost as if with foreknowledge of the coming punch line, saw I'd been not just drunk but "on a trip" I couldn't control. Years went by before I felt the useless weight of my judgment on my own heart: the war was over, that kind of behavior was of course murder. That was as far as my thought could run. And the male code: I was blind to the way it had dictated my reaction to that redneck Jayhawker bravado.

Over the weekend I nursed my hangover and sore chest, moving slowly and sleeping much. I probably had a degree of shock – but tempered by inebriation. I felt only great, empty, sad weariness, had to sleep funny because of tender ribs, simply mark time while the organism healed. Is it trauma if the putative victim says it's not? My bunkmates said nothing about the incident – (What did *that* mean? Never mind.) The weekend passed and my judgment remained unchanged. No peacemaking impulse entered my mind – to me, a "peacemaker" was still a *Colt .45* then. I thought I could count on the brass not hearing of this enlisted mess, but only time would tell. By Sunday night I was simultaneously anxious and denying it. Moose, married and living off post, would be there in the work bay bright and early tomorrow morning.

Most of that encounter is lost; it seemed remarkable later that we erstwhile combatants simply got down to work without preamble or greeting, me sweeping weekend dust in the bay, Moose going for documents from the office, the usual start-up chores. But at some point, perhaps a different day, Moose approached me with clumsy sorry talk, saying he shouldn't have "lost his temper," though he hadn't lost it, he'd found it – but I didn't say that, instead responded carefully that I'd been drunk too. We stayed delicately away from the substance of it, let it be. In accepting his apology, such as it was, I tried to be "cool." But we both spoke with obvious caution, as if through holes in a wall we couldn't see but knew was there.

This agonistic event found behavioral resolution, I see now, in subtle dominance / submission dynamics, in accordance with ethologic principles common to primate apes. Neither of us outwardly claimed the upper hand. Suspended or subdued tension, an ethologist would readily predict, would not stand for long. And indeed, practiced as I was in stuffing unpleasantness and trained early to resolve conflict by avoiding working it through, I came rather quickly to terms with Moose, thinking *Time wounds all heels*. I held to my judgment of Moose as a murderer for years. The big oaf would never change his feelings about the poor damned farmers on whose behalf he was supposedly in Korea in the first place. But what did I, "morally superior" private, know about war? Nothing at all – I'd never been shot at, except once stealing Christmas holly with Sam – but we asked for that, and anyway our lives were never really in danger from birdshot at a long distance.

But I burned with humiliation at old Casey's summary judgment of me: "couldn't pour piss out of a boot." The hell I couldn't!

War is chaos of the cosmic kind. We who haven't been there sense it rather than know it, this dauntless Galahad no less than anyone. I wondered much later if Moose had been lying, embellishing whatever had in fact happened on those morning rides to the truce line – maybe even it was a one-time event. Was the big dummy just an alcoholic blowhard, an egotistical bullshit artist, or a common bully safe in his braggadoccio because witnesses to it were dead or elsewhere? Had it happened once, or many times? What is atrocity? Who knows? How many *My Lai*s happened in Korea, Vietnam? Who knows the answer to that? The guys who were there know, but they're uncountable and unaccountable, and they ain't talking, mostly. The male code guides them toward their graves with lips forever zipped lest the abcess of their trauma dribble out for all to look at.

XI
Killing Time

Old Logan – who wasn't old, and whose mentoring initiatives I would not acknowledge for years – came along after the famous beer party and questioned me about taking leave time. He caught me off balance, under the influence of a dream from the night before. I demurred, not strongly, that I didn't need a vacation. Denial of homesickness was now part of my pattern.

The dream got to me. To call it "meaningful" didn't occur to me then – but it was odd, even disturbing. I had awakened wondering why a dream of the old railroad line running through my home town, a confused image of the tracks where once we'd lain a snake – limp and thoroughly dead at our hands – along the rail before an approaching train. We had properly marvelled at a faint stain, the only sign of the reptile we could find after the cars passed. The dream aroused a piercing nostalgia I wouldn't admit, which didn't keep it from coloring my mood for a time.

I told Logan taking leave was out of the question, I hadn't the money for such a long trip, whereupon Sarge educated me in the secrets of cadging rides on Air Force flights. Right next door at Kirtland AFB, military cargo planes, even passenger flights, took off daily headed east, and I could fly free, service policy:
They don't pay us nothin, it's the least they can do for us.

Maybe it would take several hops, he said, but I could almost surely get close to DC, maybe Langley Field, or even

Anacostia, and eat in mess halls along the way. It might take a couple days, but it would be free.

Once you got home, your folks would feed you, wouldn' they? That was a blow that hurt, but it was innocently given and I said nothing.

A few days later, the train dream occurred again in predawn hours, but this time I woke to a real train whistle coming in the bay window, of the same pitch and timbre as the dream and the real trains of my youth. Feeling foolish, I recognized its connection to the dream. A rational explanation: I need not maunder about being homesick.

But soon the notion of "catching a hop" became attractive: a deserved privilege for an élite soldier. I said something to Logan. I gave scarce thought to what "going home" actually meant, thinking not of family but myself: maybe things had changed, maybe it would be alright. I had changed, I was on my own now, doing important work.

Sure, said the Air Force desk sergeant under the Kirtland control tower, *see that guy over there? Go talk to him, he's going to Shreveport in a little while.*

The plane was an old DC-3, cargo-fitted, windowless and noisy, without upholstery to dampen vibration, no seats. I arranged a pile of parachutes and my duffel bag as cushions. Dim light filtered back from a single porthole above a jump seat holding a strapped-down box, the only evident cargo, me the only passenger. The takeoff was rough and briefly enjoyable, actually thrilling as the old crate lunged and wallowed up out of the hot desert air, soon turning into cool droning monotony, hour on hour. At some point I noticed rivets holding the aluminum skin to the frame rotating slowly in their holes. They weren't coming loose, just turning; nevertheless I was comforted by the parachutes.

Shreveport was at 107 F when we landed that evening, cloyingly steamy. I couldn't dry myself after a shower in the transient barracks. It was too late for supper in the base dining hall. I made do with beer, pretzels and pickled eggs, one beer only, knowing I had to wake myself early. I would hate to miss what might be the only flight out of that malodorous tropical armpit.

Another *Gooney Bird* hop north in beautiful weather found me before noon at Camp Campbell, Kentucky, home the 101st Airborne. The pilot told me not to stray far, we wouldn't be here long. On the tarmac as far as I could see were ranked companies of helmeted paratroops in full jump gear, chutes, field packs and rifles, standing in the sun beside huge transport planes. Time passed. It was warm. Pilot and co-pilot returned just as the paratroopers began to board planes. It was a huge operation, with many aircraft beginning to take off in close sequence. As the last Fairchild zoomed past on takeoff we got flight clearance. Up in cool air again, I watched as plane after plane emptied its human contents into balmy air over emerald green countryside, chutes blossoming and floating like milkweed seeds. The white clusters mingled with puffy clouds against deep blue, the suspended soldiers swinging to and fro. And as if on cue came a quavering accelerating exclamation-mark: a "Roman candle" streaming down through the skyful of white blossoms, freezing me in stunned shock. A parachute had opened but failed to catch air. Arrowlike it plummeted behind a forested ridge. Horrified, mind racing, I jumped up and went forward to the cabin, told the pilot and co-pilot what I had just seen, shouting above the engine roar. The pilot glanced at me and said matter-of-factly,

Yeah, we saw it. Happens all the time – this is their qualifying jump. They lose one almost every time.

Taken aback by his blasé attitude, I fixed on the thought *I just saw a man die.* The utter bizarreness of it bothered me a long time. I had seen death at close hand before – that old black fisherman on the Potomac. But this was shocking in a different way. There seemed something "permissive" about it, as if the Army had let it happen:

They plan on it, the pilot said sardonically, *they pack their own chutes.*

Sarge said later,

Sometimes they live through it, medical discharge, wheelchair the rest of their life.

Feelings predominated in my home visit. Feelings are also facts. The first incident had a kind of predictability. A day or two after arriving I took a walk up the road away from the town center, noting new houses going up everywhere. I was heading toward what used to be the open country we roamed with our .22s or fishing rods. A short distance up, I came to the old MacNamara farm with its spacious front pasture and long lane downslope to the big worn two-story house by the creek, with woods behind. At the junction of driveway and road was scrawly white graffitti, hard to read at first, suddenly stark and ugly: NIGGERS LIVE HERE. A messy arrow pointed at the lane. I stared at it, glanced at the house where no person was to be seen, and began to burn with fury that felt like pressure in my head. Straightaway I turned about face and walked swiftly back, found Dad in his easy chair, must have been a weekend, and queried him about paint thinner and a rag or old brush. My cold indignation made him look at me funny, but I got the stuff and walked back up there, and after minutes of intense activity, no traffic interrupting, I smudged the insult into illegible gray. Finished, I stood there feeling drawn toward the house – for what? To apologize? Express my anger? And then a sudden new feeling smacked me: *I don't live here any more, so why bother?* Besides, this family is new to the place, according to my Mom, perhaps hadn't even seen the graffiti yet, in which case calling it to their attention could only upset them and add to Jim Crow oppression in a country heavy enough with it. In the end, having done all I could think of, I left.

Few other trace memories remain: Grandma working her garden; the ripening plums on the driveway trees; teasing my curious Dad about what I was doing at Sandia. I managed to amplify my own importance without giving away Top Secret information, and secretly relished being "one up" on the old man. The days passed slowly. I was still susceptible to my father's monologs, more boring than ever – were that possible. And of course my siblings. How could I not delight in my new infant sister, so sensuously appealing in her warm baby fragrance? I cuddled her, a delicious pleasure – and then a quick wordless heartsick vertigo nearly stupefied me. I gave her to somebody else, limited myself, cut her off, it was too painful.

My sister of the poison ivy episode was working for a doctor as a practical aide, preoccupied caring for a terminal cancer patient in the neighborhood, a woman bleeding rectally in great quantities at the end, exhausting my sister who, when home mostly slept, her epilepsy under seeming control with phenobarbitol. My older brothers were probably working by then. I was bored – Grandma was busy in the garden, sunup to sundown, solitary, silent, uncomplaining, but always with a smile at her first-born grandson who sat reading the morning paper obsessively, even the obituaries, rather than dirty his hands weeding alongside her.

How long I stayed is gone but my departure was imminent when, leaving the house with a brother on some fun errand, thoroughly predictable tragedy struck. The day was warm and sunny, younger siblings and neighborhood kids playing everywhere. Among them was a playmate of my youngest brother, the pair of them on the front lawn. No one noticed the neighbor boy with a big-headed golf club, a driver of his father's. And no one watched him showing my littlest brother how to swing, how to drive a make-believe ball as if on a make-believe golf course, and everybody's attention was elsewhere including mine, urging my brother *Let's go*. And at that moment came the hideous sound that jerked around every head in the yard – and my littlest brother, age eight, lay felled by an impact which inset a polygon of bone the size of a half dollar into his left temple, blood weeping around the edges of the dent.

In its nature, trauma blots out detail. If severe enough, it cancels memory wholesale and the victim is said to suffer "traumatic amnesia." With psychotrauma the case is more mixed. The precipitating event may not erase all trace of narrative, but seldom can facts be reassembled into a story, regardless of effort or the sensitive empathic care of others. Whether factual stuff resurfaces and becomes articulate or remains hidden, the feeling-life of the victim is none the less permanently distorted, physically, in tissue and nerve and behavior, usually unrecognized by the isolated self. Only if that person, on faith it may be, can accept or "own" the hidden existence of sequelae to the trauma, only then may a breakthrough occur, sometimes, leading to release from chains that bind with merciless tenacity.

My little brother recovered from the injury, for which symptomatic care only was provided, and in obsessive resentment against my dad I wondered if money lay behind what seemed to me meager care for Jim. *Grand mal* epilepsy subsequently presented and followed him all his life, unnaturally shortened it. Gougingly expensive drug regimens never gave him adequate freedom from seizures. These facts speak only to the little boy himself. Any after-effects that followed on the rest of the family are unknown, but there is indication of the pain Bob Meagher, pain expert, calls "miasma."

As for me, I went back to Sandia with the horror of the "accident" stuffed, feeling I had just made my last trip home. This family was weirdly marked in a way I couldn't define. But I felt a shivery certainty that it would destroy me without remorse if I didn't stay away from it. It was not conscious perception or malicious intent to abandon my family, for it had abandoned me a long time before. For years, out of the blue, I was jerked by acute pangs that felt like being stabbed: flashbacks of that awful wet *Thwock!*

. . .

Visual memories around the ORI seem to shimmer as through rippling water. Tension among us rose as the day approached. I seemed to enter a state of high alert, became punctilious in the performance of my tasks, even on old practice warheads. I was completely ready to deal with the Real Thing and looked forward to the perceived challenge thrown before us.

We worked together on main disassembly but separated to work on sub-sections. It was not rocket science, this systematic routine of inspection, cleaning, maintenance and testing. The detonators with dummy warheads had no explosive content, hence were not dangerous; yet I carefully examined the silver wire on each contact face, looking for tarnish or a break, even handled them with both hands as protocol required with live ones. I checked their electrical resistance with focussed attention, carefully filled out log cards smudged and dog-eared with ohmage notations that had not varied over many tests by anonymous other technicians. I changed psychically as soon as the caisson was opened, assumed concentration proper to a surgical theater: alert, immediately responsive. I was rehearsing, if only for official eyes that might watch me in the ORI. If I found a resistance not within spec I told Sarge, who merely said, *Write it down.* Who knew how many hands these dummy devices had passed through?

For the weapon to work right, detonators must explode simultaneously. Yet the cables connecting them to the thyrotron were of varying length, hence the thyrotron charge would pass short cables' reach before the longer ones. To make cables the same electrical length, resistors slowed passage of the charge according to cable length. Keeping the correct cable going to the right detonator was guided by small clips which limited their motion. Yet from time to time early on, a cable was inadvertently switched, locked onto the wrong detonator. On a live weapon, the result would be lopsided implosion: a reduced and "dirty-bomb" yield.

These sad threads of fact paint a picture of habitual left-brain process. Where was I really in the waiting days before the ORI? Apart from work life, little interested me deeply or for long. I saw a movie now and then, or drank beer, went once to check out leather-working at the post Craft Shop. But the Sergeant In Charge was mainly interested in making money on tools and leather stock, for which he was the sole source, and I soon wandered away. At one point a buddy talked me into playing bingo. The emcee was a smiling talkative second lieutenant, the new Sandia Base Recreation Officer:

I'm here to give you guys something to do after hours, some good wholesome fun.

An outburst of sarcastic ridicule didn't faze him. He proceeded to lay out the rules, mixed with running patter about himself, about this barren desert he found himself in, about the poor state of the world generally, and mentioned a recent posting to Germany and how, just before returning Stateside, just why he didn't know except he felt he should, he had visited Dachau – where twelve years after liberation the stench of death was still in the air.

Twelve years and you can still smell it, can you imagine that?

Shortly I found myself with a bingo, and wended my way up front and came face to face with another guy who also had a winning card. The lieutenant solved the problem by letting us draw cards for the prize. I lost and soon left, dwelling not on "Lady Luck" but Dachau...

Of course I could not see myself as I was: a private not at all gung ho, yet who at times behaved dreamily as if he were on a "professional track." Professional track? Who was I kidding? How could there be such a thing for a private E-1? There couldn't, but there was no harm in acting "as if" for the brass. With no "fire in my gut," still I acted out the myth of belonging to an "élite" unit, aware on some shadowy level I would never be *of* it. This play-acting wore through periodically to inarticulate suspicions and dismal caged feelings, which corroded into melancholy tape-loop musings, feelings I handled by calling them names: the "blues" or the "blahs."

I got into trouble once during those waning weeks of fall. Returning one noon from the dentist, I entered the barracks before going to lunch and back to work. No one was around to observe me. That October in New Mexico was unusually congenial for outdoor swimming and the Post Pool was still open. On impulse I got my trunks, left the barracks and went up the street to the pool, got a locker and towel from the zombie attendant and enjoyed a swim with nobody around. In the brilliant heat of the desert sun, with hummingbirds sipping nectar from flowers I'd never seen before, I relaxed in the perfect luxury of stolen solitude; the more I thought about the heat of the work bay the more repellent it seemed. Nobody knew I *wasn't* at the dentist. I felt safe, my ass covered, excited to be skyving off undetected. I slept. When the sun went behind some trees the air cooled. I dressed and waited until I was sure the guys in the barracks wouldn't notice anything. The cadre could be counted on to have left for the day. I slipped easily into barracks routine and went to chow.

The next morning I couldn't get out of bed. I panicked. I knew what sunburn was, but had never roasted myself like this. I told my bunkmates I couldn't work, I couldn't even get up. Helpfully they razzed me with Army boilerplate: incapacitating sunburns were damage to "US Government Property" and I could be court-martialled for this.

Just fuck off! I groaned, on my belly, the damage mainly to my back and legs. And I got away with it, though not without a stern warning and lecture from Logan, whose expression I'd never seen so hard.

XIII
The Brink

Memory is always complicated by circumstance, meaning here the stern rigor of military secrecy. If one lives under the watchful if inept eyes of an official security apparatus, it takes heretical[5] rebelliousness to methodically retain memory of "forbidden" matters. My rebellion was inner, devious and clumsy – like that middle-of-the-day swim, illicit only because the damned sunburn betrayed me. There were no "whistleblowers;" that usage was not current then. It would be hard to make a case that columnists like Winchell and Pearson were "anti-establishment rebels." I'd never heard of I. F. Stone, of course. But integral to whistleblowing is that the person is an insider; Stone was not one. He reported from outside material, documented by official sources, to a public that couldn't care less. I knew nothing of the Constitution then, or of open democratic ways and processes – I'd left all that behind, perhaps wittingly, on swearing the oath. Thus my rebelliousness was essentially sterile, unlike I. F. Stone's.

Dry desert days colorlessly succeeded each other in the time-honored way of military life. "Spartan" was too pretentious a term for it: rise, "shit-shave-shower-shine," make your bunk, go for SOS[6] at the mess hall, get security badge, off to the work bay. Coffee break, boisterous or dull, lunch at noon, back to work, off at 4, go for a beer before chow, pick up clean laundry, take another shower if the day was really hot, then back to the beer hall or a movie, in bed by midnight. Where was my feeling life?

What was this patient, observant, beer-drinking bullshit artist really doing? I was watching, storing, stuffing the criminal insanity I was immersed in – and taking no notes.

Perhaps it was psychological projection that let me see rising tension as the ORI approached. But maybe not. There were signs outside myself, visible in the barracks as well as the work bay; it couldn't all be me. I recognized at some point that Mr. Yardley's escalating praise of us "experts" was excessive, overdone. We were no experts. Our crew chief was just pumping us up. OK technicians yes, skillful even and scrupulously careful, but this whole operation was essentially donkey-work, simple cut and dried routines performed so often we could have done them in our sleep – heaven forbid! Logan was less wordy with us, quietly solid, comradely, un-sergeant-like, a lifer long used to the riveting lockstep of SOP, comfortable with it, calmly prepared to interpret it for a greenhorn.

Yes, there are stakes, real ones, to this stuff.
What are they? What does that mean?
Means we'll be a line outfit if we pass, qualified, could be sent anywhere they need us, Germany, wherever.

This notion upset me. Being sent overseas would be like starting over somehow.

Don' worry, Germans are just like us, most of em speak English – and they've got the best beer in the world. I could not believe Germans were "just like us," feeling hair on my neck rise at Sarge's summary opinion, thinking of that Rec Officer at bingo. But I couldn't readily counter Logan's blithe assurance – Sarge had been there, seen Germans up close.

People are people regardless. I wanted to believe that, and actually did; but the monstrous revelations of German behavior – millions gassed, cremated and machine-gunned – had taken firm lodging in my mind as I was reaching the "age of reason" – or at least the age of reading newspapers, but not to the point of realizing that Poles, Hungarians, Serbs, Croats, Bulgarians, Romanians, Russians and Ukrainians also participated enthusiastically in the slaughter of Jews and other "defectives." Sensing my ignorance, I couldn't argue with Logan, nobody's fool, so I said nothing more, let it drop. The possibility of orders for Germany remained a threat in my mind, held little promise of anything like adventure.

Real-world warning of the coming inspection presented itself. We were sent to Base Security to be re-photographed. I wondered why and Logan said,
New badges.
Why?
Maybe just for show – wanna impress the inspecting team.

We had practiced our methodical operation until we were blue in the face, until anticipation became a pall of mind-bending boredom, fatigue and sagging morale. No acting out, no misbehavior, just morose dogface soldiers bitching and moaning – and a tormenting itch to get the damned thing over with. Endlessly we were told we were good, that this would be a piece of cake, no sweat GI. Probably nothing could have tranquilized us. The Colonel was seen more frequently, here and there, sauntering into a bay unexpectedly, looking for who knew what, leaving quickly with a vaguely positive remark, a permanent smile on his smooth pink cheeks. The Battalion was up to full strength with a newly assigned sergeant who would deal with electronics and would conduct the test of the Mark 6 radar during the ORI. With him came a nuclear man, drafted out of college but only a private – of all things! – who would go from bay to bay during the ORI, installing cone assemblies, real ones of plutonium, not the lead dummies we'd played with for so long. We dawdled in gray nullity, ignorant of how the inspection would proceed, where or when. Dealing with a spike of anxiety during coffee-break one morning, possibly hung-over, I voiced a sarcastic suspicion that maybe we were being inspected "at this very moment." Maybe this endless lack of information, this interminable waiting around was part of it, to see if we could hack tension like we might have to face some day. Immediate guffaws from Moose and Red,

Naw – the fuckin Army ain't that smart.

What makes you think they give a shit about us, huh? said Red.

Take it easy – this from Logan, staring mournfully at his crew.

A day or so later, ever observant, passing the office and overhearing Mr. Ford murmuring to Yardley, I was sure I heard "The weapons are in." I was instantly on the *qui vive*. A few minutes later at coffee Yardley, his demeanor totally different, was giving us his now-standard morning pep talk, saying we had nothing to worry about, we were good, we could do this job with one hand tied behind our backs. Pausing until he had eye contact with us, he enunciated in a few terse words that we should wear fresh fatigues that morning, saying mildly, as if it were of only passing importance,

We're going to Manzano next Monday morning, eight sharp, to get familiar with the bays, no tools, there'll be tools already there, same setup as here, all you need to bring is yourselves. And no matches. They'll make you empty your pockets at the gate. Might as well leave your smokes here too – no way to light up. We'll be back here by noon.

The ORI will be out there? I was thinking again about live nuclear weapons so close to the city; the Manzano mountains were not that far away.

You bet. Yardley had nothing more for us, except that we would go to Manzano in six-bys from the motor pool. And so we did.

We emptied out at a guardhouse in a deep canyon surrounded by high brown hills, their crests gilded by the rising sun. We showed badges to the MP, emptied our pockets to prove nothing incendiary within, were let through a high chainlink fence plastered with red, white and blue signs warning bilingually of the dire consequences of attempted unauthorized entry. The building – there were more than one in this compound – had a bay exactly like the one we were used to, a replica copy equipped with every tool and object we had ever laid hands on at Sandia – except that these tools seemed brand new, never used. Moose bitched about the brand of torque wrench he would use. We wandered around in the morning chill, had no questions for Yardley, who kept asking if anything we might need was missing.

The momentous event came quickly after that. Probably I appeared normal to my mates that morning, though I moved with a sort of careful precision – not trancelike, but with no wasted motion, stiff, wary at the prospect of Authority peering over my shoulder, the whole crew remote from each other, even Sarge, our usual start-up chatter quiet in the dry, faintly chemical fustiness of the bay, a strange place and yet not at the same time, the same chain hoist and benches, the same tool racks arranged the same way on the walls. Moose was still sneering at the torque wrench he'd have to use. We found the latrine, the water fountain, the supply room. We "milled about," Mr. Yardley having not yet arrived.

When a trout snaps up a dry fly, or when quail flush from cover or a rabbit dashes, there feels little separation between one's perception and reaction, according to whether the unfolding event is quick or unhurried. But there are times when the conjunction of awareness and response seems to widen, the interval blurs, partakes of a kind of elasticity: act and consequence seem to unfold over a timeless duration, seconds or eons, no way to tell. How long we stood around is not recorded. Probably the other crews were in a similar condition, everybody waiting for official start-up. Yardley seemed not to know the scenario any better than we did; he kept leaving the bay and returning with equivocal words that added up to "Not yet." The inspector was said to be a full bird colonel; lower-ranking officers would be with him. Preparations for the operation had yet to begin when there was muttering about the coffee break we were missing because of "this shit."

What is going on?
Is this fucking ORI really going to happen?
Today?

Reality congealed. Suddenly but not dramatically there were two caissons for us to roll into the bay. We lowered the steel door again. Mr. Yardley gathered us, speaking in almost hushed tones while we huddled, not circled but semi-sprawled along the spotless work-bench, looking at him at the opposite end as he mouthed mild words that seemed peculiarly not to carry across the intervening space, although we understood him well enough. His expression was calm, his body language conveying – was it "solidarity"? – something not seen in him before, perhaps stronger than that, not exactly declarative intimacy, but an unmistakable assertion: we're in this together. Then he nodded at us. We entered measuredly into the job, began our careful obeisance to nihilism. The arched olive drab cover was stencilled *4A SWD Killeen TX* and dated in yellow paint. Translation: "Fourth Army Special Weapons Depot Killeen Texas." The real thing.

The second caisson contained the tail section of the bomb, required for the complete assembly and operational test of this live Mark 6 Mod 7. But if that were true, why would we not test two particular components of the tail section? Yardley said the "spoiler baffles" and "hydraulically retracted fin" were strictly Air Force concerns. These aerodynamic modifications to the sleek dart were meant to slow its descent lest it reach ground zero before its internal machinery quickened the bomb. An Air Force crew was responsible for those details.

But why were bombs an Army job anyway?
Because we're still in AFSWP.

Mostly silent at first, casual talk arose, carefully, no jokes, just subdued prudent remarks as if we might be being overheard. We avoided the beer-drinking, card-game banter of easier days, the four of us sinking into focus, systematically taking apart precision hideousness, separating subassemblies with socket wrench or screwdriver, eventually separating the electronics to clean the golden spring fingers completing the fiendish circuit, moving deliberately, taking our time, seeming to move in the way of deep sea divers, stopping periodically to stand and look at one another, as if with a deep breath we could dissipate a newly-manifest heaviness in the dry atmosphere, contemplating, silently then aloud, why this fully equipped secret installation out here in the barren hills was so *still*.

Where is everybody? Logan, pausing, opined that since the ORI was our business, we hardly needed the rest of the battalion on hand – still, the quiet was puzzling.

Where are the inspectors?

Mr. Yardley kept leaving the bay, and once I thought I saw a frown on his face.

Red, returning from the pisser, reported meeting a lieutenant in the hall he'd never seen before, carrying a clipboard. So this is it; they were on the premises, it could happen any time now. But nobody showed up and we worked on toward disassembly, following SOP, the sub-sections spread out, the warhead now "harmless." We fell to our handmaiden tasks, measuring resistances, inspecting detonators, degreasing the cone mechanism, breathing sweetish TCE vapors, not touching one another, at times huddled around the device resting on its cradle at belt height, the four of us a team and feeling like a team, working with a trace of weightless hesitation perhaps perceptible to a sensitive observer – had one been present. And still no inspectors showed up. We seemed after a while to move as if the atmosphere had imperceptibly densified. We slid into deepening silence, staying with our tasks, absorbed in the soft clink of tools, self-confident, team-confident, anxiety stiffening us with a slightly forced respectful air, as if an inspector invisible to us was already in the bay while we wondered Where are the damned inspectors?

Take a break, men, said Yardley softly, and when we hesitated, knowing there'd be no real break, he said,

Hold up a minute, and left the bay. We stood tools in hands, on edge now, wondering if our boss would come back with the inspection team, but he returned silent, his expression set.

Any sign of them?

He gave a bare shake of his head but said nothing; quick apprehension ran around the crew. We were in midstream now, could not stop, the protocol forbad leaving a weapon open and disassembled longer than necessary. We were into it, we had to continue. It was warm now, late-morning sun beating on the high metal roof. The jackscrew mechanism for cone insertion was ready for remounting to accept the nuclear cone. The new man Private Yevry came in, placed the cone on the bench, inside the cave of lead bricks stacked earlier. He stood waiting as Sarge cleaned the inside of the appalling cavity with tissues, wearing rubber gloves for the first time ever, dropping used *Kimwipes* and gloves into the paper bag held by Yevry, the air now reeking with solvent. Moose stood by with anti-seize lubricant to insure that the jackscrews would insert the cone smoothly, fully and tightly. The NiCad batteries showed correct voltage. Our nerves tightened as the moment for insertion came. The radar man poked his head in; Yardley nodded at him.

And still no inspectors showed up to observe our progress toward the dark culmination. There was no way to fake anything, were that remotely in our heads. If we deliberately interrupted the work rhythm until "official visitors" arrived, that might itself result in a demerit, perhaps indicating other lapses in protocol. "No shortcuts today." Every single thing in proper sequence. In my taut suspension, my head seemed to float off and watch the proceedings as if gravity had somehow idiotically relaxed. The intricate electro-mechanical scenario of arming played through my mind. Super-alert, tuned to inspectors who might enter any minute, I was fixed on keeping cool, to show no trace of frivolity. What if we got a negative rating? What if we were deemed Not Operationally Ready? Raucously self-derisive about being "élite troops" as we were, still we understood we were stepping up to the plate.

Thus, tucked away in an arid canyon in secret desert hills, mindlessly groping potential apocalypse, this cobbled-together crew, cocooned in military insularity, added our essential bit to the poisoned heart of priapic nationalism, contributing our small exacting energies to its metastasizing immensity. I knew little factual about the scope of this dreadful operation, as a Regular Army volunteer from Virginia, bright and articulate but self-involved, good man but moody – *"reads too much"* – now nodding to my crew boss, "Nothing wrong" with the elegant detonators I've just finished testing for their electrical suitability.

Yardley stepped out once more, telling us again,
Hold up.

Central to my tension that day was not that I was there in the first place, knowingly serving death, abetting mass annihilation. I was holding on, trying to project sanity I sensed as illusory while warped and debilitated by awful knowledge – and an indelible shame I could not name, hence could not face.

The jackscrew mechanism was attached and bolted to the warhead, Moose emitting little grunts with his torque-wrench exertion. Logan fitted the nuclear cone and started to connect cables, his face inches from the plutonium. We brought the electronics forward, carefully mating the gold spring fingers to the contact ring. Now ready for reassembly, tension rose palpably when Yardley went to find the electronics sergeant who would verify functioning of the bomb's radar trigger. Our chief was gone noticeably longer than before, and returned agitated and red-faced, saying loudly,

There's nobody here!

We're here, somebody said, but the humor died before Yardley's scowl.

What about the other crews? said Logan.

Ford's crew is finished already – just standing around. There's not one single officer in this whole compound but me!

Where's Mister Ford ?

His men said he left, said he had to go make a bank deposit! But there's no CO, no Exec Officer, no officers at all, and no sign of any inspection team whatsoever.

Why not? I said.

Those bastards, those chickenshit bastards!

We knew instantly what he meant, and Warrant Officer Yardley's full-blown fury swept his men along.

They're afraid of us! They think we're gonna blow them up! They think we don' know what the fuck we're doin'! He continued to rant until we began to feel uncomfortable. Abruptly noticing the effect of his anger on his men, Yardley brought himself back to the moment. Here was a partially-assembled live Mark 6 to button up and put through its paces. This was *ORI* and he was damned if those gutless wonders would keep him from doing his job.

And so it unrolled. Thyrotron and batteries were cabled up. Maneuvering with extra care now, we were jittery with suppressed feeling at our isolation, at Yardley's outburst. Moose scowlingly installed detonators. The electronics sergeant looked in the door, gauging our readiness then leaving again. Private Yevry left as well, saying "Don't worry," meaning he would be back to retrieve the cone assembly when it was over. And then we were installing the curved outer plates shaping the bomb's profile, bolting on the tail, and then the weapon was a teardrop whole except for the fiberglass nose cone containing the radar antenna, dangling by its cable. We waited for the radar man, standing immobile at various points around the weapon, out of the way, Logan in front ready to pick up the nose cone and aim it at the sergeant, who entered with his meter, walked around in front of the bomb and stationed himself near the outer bay door. Logan, checking faces all around, pushed the red *Manual Insert* button: the worm gears squealed into grinding exertion: the motor was working under bomb power now, arming was going forward, criticality was now possible, and the awful moment arrived. The jackscrews groaned abruptly to a halt: the cone was seated. Twenty or thirty or forty thousand tons' worth of exponential hell sat balanced on its dolly. We stood stock still, locked on in those crackling seconds. No fail-safe disconnect existed. All this bomb needed was a few microseconds of the right kind of radar reflection. One man realized he was holding his breath: I was now light-headed. We were all gripped by the indescribable potential we had meticulously brought to this moment. We were utterly hushed, as if no matter how exquisitely snail-like careful we'd been, as if through some tiny inadvertence, some forgotten or insignificant or unnoticed or unsuspected perturbation or random sneak circuit in the complex electronics on the way to this all-or-nothing moment might terminate in a noiseless and signless nothingness, which if it were to happen there would be no last cascading gooseflesh to make us stare stone-rigid into each others' terrible eyes.

Several eons later the impassive radar man, him of alleged 170 IQ, nodded almost-bored confirmation that this bomb was absolutely what it was.

XIV
Abandoned

Psychic pain gripped me night and day: betrayal. It was the ripping away of dare I say rose-colored scales from eyes dreamily unconcerned with life as it is. Ever consciously averse to daily realities of power and dominance, I was stunned when I got it. I reeled in boiling inward hurt which fumed up in cold rage I could pour out to no one:

Lieutenants are first out of the trenches.

The captain goes down with the ship if anybody else remains aboard.

If you don't have esprit de corps you've got a mob, not an army.

This was plain fucking cowardice, cutting and running at the critical moment; these bastards showed their true colors, leaving enlisted men alone with a fully armed live nuclear weapon while they scurried off on personal errands that just happened to take them away from what could be Ground Zero.

Anger in A Company was general, the other crews bitching and mocking the absconding officers. Their bitterness validated my own bleak fury. Later I felt proud of Yardley for sticking with us. The betrayal – no other word fit what I felt – mocked our vaunted "collegiality," made a fatuous mockery of our self-regard: "élite troops" indeed. However, calming down, I indulged my feelings aloud only so long as others did, and when they adapted, so did I outwardly, not failing to notice the effect of my continuing passion, visible more than verbal, on my mates, who noted my descent into bitter silence.

The discontent in A Company didn't produce anything close to insurrection; the modern US Army is no freeholder militia. And no real damage was done us. My resentment had no tinge of class consciousness – I sought privilege as eagerly as anyone, maybe more than most.

However the ascendancy of feeling over fact in the aftermath besmears narrative. Morosely we went back to work the next day, the letdown multiplied by hangovers. My dispirited introspection left few traces in memory. It was not in me to be detached, let alone philosophical about the debacle, unlike Logan who greeted us next morning with ironic surprise, trying to lift spirits,

Well, we're all here today! His humor fell flat – I simmered in my bitterness. Insofar as I could identify what I felt – though feelings didn't matter – "abandoned" comes close. This was followed in time by cynical acceptance: "We're all in this alone." I had bought into this cold-blooded impersonal barbarity by turning away from the truth of Manning and Branch. I had yet to learn that courage is an emergent quality, often latent and unpredictable in nature. I had no thought of transferring out of the Fourteenth this far into the game. But I was wakening to madness.

It was a long time before I could look calmly at the "cowardly" officer behavior in the ORI. If a crew should mess up and touch off a Mark 6, hypothetically possible, then the fewer human beings at ground zero the better. The cadre weren't cowards, they were pragmatic, went the argument, and there was nothing whatever heroic about this stepwise, straightforward process. Our officers trusted our skill and competence. Had they not, "We'd have stayed around," as Mr. Ford loudly retorted to Mr. Yardley's acid probing. The encounter between the two Warrant Officers warmed and delighted my authoritarian heart; Yardley was "on our side." Backhandedly we turned our derision into pride: "We did the job without the fuckin' brass snooping on us." Besides, who knew, maybe AFSWP had ordered all superfluous personnel out of the area. No way to learn about that. It would be decades before General Lee Butler, delving into the dense secrecy of the nuclear enterprise, fully showed us the hideous fruits of moral nihilism gone global.

What about the ORI itself – had it been real? Was it official? Where were those no-show inspectors? What was that all about? Logan shrugged; there was no one else I could turn to, no way to address what still felt like abandonment weeks later. No one used that word of course; we weren't abandoned, only felt like it, therefore we should stuff it. Bleakly I wondered whether it had even been an ORI. Nothing had come from Headquarters about it – for security reasons? And somebody said the Colonel was not even around for the big day because he was preparing for an important trip to the Pentagon the following day. Meaning: he was around but had not joined his men in their test. Weeks later, smolderingly scornful at any notion we were now "professionals," I simply asked Yardley whether we had in fact passed the ORI. The crew chief stared at me with a trenchant pause. I let myself be satisfied with his terse affirmative. So we were now ready for "line duty" – where?

On the Friday night I attained my majority I happened to mention the fact to George Coleman, a strong and very black supply corporal from the Big Peedee River, who immediately went to his locker and returned with a half-pint of *Jose Cuervo* tequila, insisting I take it:

Happy birt'day man! Dis is good stuff, man, have it!

After a spasm of shy and effusive thank-yous at his totally unexpected gesture, I opened the bottle, but on an impulse insisted George have the first drink, which caused him a spasm

too, shy embarassment I didn't recognize at first as delight poorly concealed: he tried to cover up, saying,
It's foh you, man, have it, happy birt'day!

Puzzled, thinking "on my feet" so to speak, I saw what this dancing repartée meant: if George took the first swig, then gave it back to me, I would be a white man sharing the same bottle black lips had touched. Maybe this was the first time George had been in that position in his life! I held out the flask unwaveringly. He finally took a little sip, then I did and we talked, George settling on the bunk beside me, the bay deserted. Soon we were hashing over the 14th Ordinance Battalion, our new company commander and the Army in general. George said the Army was home for him. He couldn't live in Carolina or he might probably be dead by now, this Army was no piece of cake either, but his boss Kayo was not all that bad.

No longer feeling like a professional warrior, and saddened by George's notion of the Army as community or family, I spoke not of my own past, not knowing George that well. I kept nipping on the fierce liquor and fell to bitching about the ORI. George said he didn't really know what A Company did, and he liked it that way. End of conversational mutuality. Declining more tequila, he said he was going downtown, was sorry there wasn't salt and lemon to go with the tequila, you needed salt and a cut lemon to make it perfect, and after awhile our talk flattened out and trailed away, the bottle empty. George went downtown as he did most weekends, denying he had a girl friend but often not returning till reveille Monday morning.

At two in the morning, this cactus juice initiate awoke still dressed, needing to pee. I could hardly find my way to the latrine. The next morning, Saturday, brought the worst headache of my entire life.

In those post-ORI weeks I slowly accepted my mental writhing. It was a matter of feelings only, strictly mine to deal with. I understood the Army now, absolutely and forever, and I bent myself toward 'sticking it out' – this enlistment would definitely come to an end.

The battalion was in limbo as well, awaiting assignment. Colonel Healy retreated to higher echelon and seemed to vanish. Logan mentioned one day he didn't want to go back to Germany, he had been there, and said he thought the CO didn't either. But that wouldn't matter if the Pentagon chose to send us there. Sarge himself could – and would – transfer out of the 14th, having enough service longevity to get a Stateside assignment easily. Later he spoke of a 12th Ordnance Battalion I had never heard of. It seemed that months ago, a grease gun[7] had disappeared from the arms room of this 12th Battalion and was later traced by serial number to a band of guerillas deep in the Cuban mountains. Knowing nothing about the tyrant Batista, the story stuck in my memory only because I couldn't imagine our own punctilious supply sergeant letting a grease gun get away from him that way. When I said as much, Logan nodded. The 12th was soon to be disbanded, he said, but it had nothing to do with the theft. What his remarks did pertain to directly was Private Barry and the hallowed off-the-record Army system of local resource allocation called "cumshaw" by the enlisted ranks: say a quartermaster has a ton of toilet paper on hand for some reason, but needs the space it occupies to receive an imminent shipment of paint, or field tents or C-rations. He may shop around for another supply man low on asswipe, who might have something useful to the first, some welcome item which would not take up room needed for the incoming. Thus a mutually beneficial exchange may be struck between them. Learning from Sarge that the 14th was trading with the 12th, and having agreed to work one day with Sergeant Kayo cleaning and stacking stuff in the dim basement supply room, I happened to observe close-order conversation between Kayo and another sergeant who came along, their talk conducted in low but not furtive voices. I couldn't tell what either one was offering or wanted from the other, or even that it was cumshaw barter, their speech indistinct and unhurried. But then Kayo left, went upstairs and returned shortly with the battalion Top Sergeant, who reported directly to the colonel. Discussion resumed and became somewhat animated but still in low tones. The strange sergeant, from the 12th Battalion it would shortly emerge, seemed to be resisting whatever the proposed deal was. Our two sergeants were clearly bending paired persuasive powers on him. After a long time the visitor seemed to give in, and hearing clearly for the only time in the session, I was jarred by Kayo's words:

…but only if you take Barry too…
Aw man, gimme a break! came the response, and then,
Sweeten it a little for Chrissakes.
What ya need?
Yellow paint.
All I got is one gallon.
Aw, man…

Murmured conversation continued between the three non-coms for several minutes. Then our Sergeant Major left and went back upstairs, and by the weekend, outcast Private Barry had gotten orders and departed the 14th Ordnance Battalion forever.

Traded for a gallon of yellow paint! was the way it came out at coffee break later, amid savage laughter. A silent eavesdropper, I was glad I had told no one what I witnessed and wondered who started this story, which was inaccurate, backwards and only one part of the basement deal I had witnessed. I didn't correct the guy telling the story, and never learned the main focus of the barter session. The fate of Private Barry had seemed secondary from my perspective, but maybe it wasn't. However I felt glad it had happened, blind to my scapegoating impulse. But I wondered how often such decisions took place below the awareness of the brass. If it could happen to Barry, it could happen to me – or anyone. What use to keep your nose clean when these guys had such power?

I cain't make you do a damn thing, but I can sure as hell make you wish you had! came back to me...

As if standing beside myself, I suddenly saw my isolation: by sticking to myself and steering deliberately away from loose gossip or even ordinary chow-line banter, I might be, probably was, missing "useful information." Now I understood another level of Army life hitherto hidden, scary even though this intrigue had solved a company problem. Perhaps the brass had discussed with their NCOs what to do with Barry. Sergeant Major Caslin surely had not forged the Colonel's signature on the transfer orders that Personnel drew up.

A round of promotions happened after the ORI, and in my solitude I had no way to know if I was passed over because of the sunburn incident. Perhaps that played no part, but I suspected it had. I felt left behind, but was not assertive enough to ask Logan why I hadn't made Pfc when guys with less seniority had.

The documentation is there, if sketchy. The paper on which orders were mimeographed is now brittle and brownish yellow, still readable despite random ink blots. Perhaps it was forecast that I would save paperwork laid on me by the Army, indicating self-protective caution which mixed paranoia with my self-absorption. I kept the papers in a folio in my footlocker, but always fickle of mood, I lost or discarded many of them, even while believing I might one day need them. The Top Secret aura of Sandia life actively inhibited thinking about eventualities for which these papers might be useful. This seems borne out by the orders I did manage to hold onto. I couldn't have specified why I retained the sketchy file – perhaps only a hazy notion of "posterity." Underlying my ruminations were lingering romantic feelings I'd have repudiated if questioned. Yet, whether I was an élite troop or a dogface soldier, I understood I was at the heart of something vast and ominous.

One lost document is a Signal Corps photo of a Major shaking hands with me, some temporary Battalion Exec, his name gone, taken on the occasion of this volunteer private embarassed by being named "Soldier of the Month" for January 1955. I was so revolted by the tepid hamminess of the image that I tore the 8 x 10 glossy into little pieces. But I retained the "Letter of Commendation" signed by the Colonel. It says,

1. This is to congratulate you on your being selected as the Soldier of the Month for January 1955. Your active interest in the organization and creditable attention to duty has been deeply appreciated both by me and your immediate supervisors.

2. It is indeed a pleasure to have a soldier of your initiative and ability assigned to this organization. Your actions characterize a true soldier of the United States Army and reap credit not only upon yourself and this battalion, but on the Service as a whole.

3. A copy of this letter will be placed in your Field Military 201 File.

Well, I didn't kiss any ass to get it, I retorted when guys razzed me about the award, unaccompanied of course by tangible compensation. I refused to show the commendation to anybody. I was right about the brown-nosing – as a general rule I stayed as far from officers as I could and still be in A Company. Later I thought the award might be a "consolation prize" in lieu of a Pfc stripe.

XV
Aftermath

After the ORI ordeal, a bifurcation of mind became apparent: I was a soldier, but an atomic one. This adjectival dichotomy became a cold heavy fact: that ORI bomb went back on line, ready to use. It marked initiation into the heart of the nuclear complex; a threshold had been crossed. I was now indisputably complicit. The nuclear Army had sucked me into a mindset not dissimilar from that of the wreakers of European genocide. I could not endure contemplating that chilling awareness for long – that would have amounted to obsession. Absolution was out of the question. Unable to articulate my feelings, there was no relief, no sympathetic ear, certainly no damned sky-pilot[8] and thus no solace for an increasing burden. Sandia was no longer *terra incognita*. I now knew all anybody needed to know, and in fact had since Bob Manning's inquisitory bluntness. He was right, and it was a mixture of unwillingness and inability to look at this dark immersion straight on. I was not conscious of guilt; going along to get along had no moral dimension. My evasion was not "unmanly." I resorted to no exculpatory blather, found no justification in such abstractions as "concern for the greater good." My complicity was a reality; I swallowed it, knowing I had to live with it.

Trauma was only a medical term: my little brother's golf-club accident, or that Roman-candling paratrooper. It didn't occur to me that a burnt, pounded or torn body poses an enormous problem for its brain unless death should supervene. The notion of *psycho*trauma was beyond my ken, never mind the quaintly imprecise military notion of "shell shock." I wondered not about the *psychic* struggles of survivors to heal themselves. In the antiseptic milieu of the 14th Ordnance Battalion (Special Weapons), the forgotten horror of Hiroshima and Nagasaki receded, became phantasmal morbid imaginings merely "hypothetical." Swallowing nuclear reality was but another feat of denial.

It was as difficult in those days and that time to feel ill will toward one's government as toward one's parents or doctor or – for *some* – pastor. Did I "believe in" the Army, the way one accepts medicine, or law, or Coca-Cola? Definitely not; I would have said I "saw through" the military. Perhaps there was ethical courage in me somewhere. I might even have admitted so if asked in a certain manner. But this battalion was not living out some hard-ass scenario of victory after supreme struggle. No projections of bloody heroism animated the 14th. There was no Audie Murphy or Sergeant York bullshit. We were nuclear technicians. If I was aware of the inhuman remoteness that warmaking was becoming, as Manning had warned, that chilling prospect was balanced by assurance of the improbability of war: deterence. This battalion would never be called to desperate exploits of arms; such a reality was far below any of our consciousnesses. And so I abided the picayune privileges of my "élite" status.

Yet I found myself fumbling through spells of inominate sorrow, a shapeless anguish that eventually jelled into formless yearning. These were not attacks of homesickness: I had left my father's house. Conscious self-pity had germinated by now, but was not yet ascendant. I quickly turned away from the past, could not admit sustenance from the sorts of memories others found nostalgically warm. The past was trivial and repulsive, musty beyond any hope of joy.

In the other part of my life, as GI, as barracks soldier, I behaved in conventional ways. Enlisted men piss and moan freely about Army chow, although AFSWP fed its personnel lavishly by infantry standards, better than anything I had known growing up. And along with everybody else I bitched and whined about low pay, stingy supply sergeants, perpetual hurry-up-and-wait. I was ever ready to swill beer and swap greenhorn lies much tamer than the war stories of the company lifers. Bored, restless, quick to seize diversion in the sterile march of days, wanting action, any kind of grab-ass, organized or not, I snatched at any opportunity to skyve off if I thought I could get away with it.

I fell in with a buddy who introduced me to a new Tennessee bourbon called "sour mash." By then I'd gone to Personnel and cancelled the allotment deducted from my pay to send home for the wrecked Dodge. I never finished paying off that loan secured by my father.

Urged on by this new buddy, a draftee savagely scornful of the "fuckin Army," I went diffidently to our new Company Commander and in a conversation that was remarkably mutually affable, asked the Captain to co-sign a loan so I could buy a certain high-powered rifle. He assented so easily I was suspicious for a moment, but only a moment. The downtown dealer took the promissory note, my down payment, and gave me the rifle. My buddy already had a rifle. Shortly we left Albuquerque in a decrepit old Ford and spent a long cold Saturday out on the *Llano Estacado*, me wondering what the name meant, figuring something must have happened here since it was inscribed broadly across the road map. Later I learned the Spanish means "Staked Plains," which didn't tell me any more about this great expanse of many square miles sprawling beyond the Pecos River, mute witness to great suffering and death when Kit Carson's cavalry mercilessly ravaged the Navaho homeland and drove hundreds of Indians down to Bosque Redondo below Fort Sumner in bitter cold, deep snow and starvation rations.

That country unaccountably and illogically seemed somehow high in elevation, as if it were the broad crown of some vast mesa invisible because limitless. The empty grasslands seemed elevated above mountains, never mind we'd left mountains far behind. The altitude sensation was doubtless self-generated; yet it seemed to be transmitted from the ground itself. What is certain is the desolation of the *Llano* that day: nothing but sky and thick blond grass and a chill northwest wind. We stayed within sight of the car, perhaps subliminally awe-struck by the vastness of the space we roved, some yards abreast. We took notice when a shapeless overcast began to dim the sun, which seemed a tiny dot starting to depart as if on a trip. Soon we needed the dark mark of the Ford in the graying distance to keep oriented in a landscape increasingly featureless. We met no other soul that day, but if we had, and had that person happened to mention the "spirits of this place," one of us would have grinned half-embarassed and looked at the ground while the other might have attempted a poker face to cover what would otherwise be seen as a sneer. I would never have admitted the possibility then, but perhaps my contempt for the spiritual was "cover," the flip side of a quality as indigenous to humans as their hairy armpits. We erstwhile sharpshooters were of course completely, Americanly ignorant of the bloody history of our hunting ground.

Soon we were noisily firing at long range at poised or racing jackrabbits, challenging targets on the endless grassland. We were just starting to get the hang of it when our cartridges ran out. Eating our proceeds was mooted by living in barracks, though to speak plainly, those high-velocity bullets would have meant skilful trimming to salvage good meat from macerated flesh. Anyway jackrabbits weren't game, just varmints, notwithstanding they were welcome fare to local folk in Depression times, before war and oil and uranium began to subvert whole populations into consumptive dependence on the military-industrial complex. We let the long-legged bounders lay where they fell, almost. We gathered a number of them, hung them on a barbed wire fence and photographed them. That snapshot has not survived.

I had to give the rifle to Sergeant Kayo for "safe-keeping" in the Arms Room, which put me in the position of having to converse with him when I wanted to use it. Kayo was soft-spoken and outwardly pleasant, but a hard-pants soldier all the same. I couldn't warm up to him, remembering his role in getting rid of Private Barry – I had gotten the message of that incident, somewhat. I can't call Kayo ruthless, but that's what the episode amounted to. I was reflexively wary around him afterward. I thought we'd had a break-through conversation about racism early in our acquaintance, but part of my unease, as I surrendered the rifle that Monday morning, was a certain "wondering" about our first conversation, remembering it only as "a bit strange." I recalled ambiguous phrases and Corporal Coleman's carefully indirect remark about his boss, as well as hard-to-read expressions on the face of this clearly intelligent man only a couple years older than me. My notion of racism did not include how hard it would ever be for a black American to actually trust any white man. Nor could I see my own white privilege, the unaware entitlement that mantled me quite apart from the bigotry I had repudiated all my life.

XVI
Deer Hunting

My new Jack Daniels buddy learned of a cabin in the woods up north, said we could use it during the forthcoming deer season. It was owned by the AFSWP Headquarters Top Sergeant, who converted his company's dayroom into a true casino every payday after work, running blackjack, poker and dice games with the help of enlisted subordinates who might be called "accomplices" today. Thousands of dollars changed hands those rowdy Friday nights. An MP from our own B Company won enough to buy a new *Pontiac V8 "Starchief"* in two hours of blackjack. Perhaps aware how basic gambling was to my character, I gave in to peer pressure one payday and went over to Headquarters that night. I had no intention of playing and only went out of curiosity. One look into the crowded, noisy casino and I left and never went back, recognizing a set-up which was anything but gambling.

This military impresario was a true if petty tyrant, hated by everybody below him in rank, according to my buddy, who had managed to get use of the cabin by being near-perfect in his clerical job, and by shrewdly manipulating the Top Sergeant's abyssal ignorance of the world beyond Army life.

The cabin was a one-room shack with steel Army bunks in a forest of immense pines in the Jemez Mountains west of Los Alamos. That forest is radically changed now, by chain-saw massacre or holocaust born of fire-suppression. Windowless, the cabin had a rusty sheet-metal stove for which we clumsily scrounged deadwood in the dark. *You didn' bring a fuckin flashlight?*

We evicted a family of white-footed mice from the sooty inside and warmed ourselves enough to take off field jackets. We numbered four, all draftees but me. I had never met the two new guys. Ignorant as I was, they thought I was the most woods-wise of us. We ate macaroni and cheese, drank beer and Jack Daniels. Later, stretching out and feeling good, housekeeping chores done, we saw to our rifles and ammo and knives, as if to convince ourselves and each other we knew what the hell was going on: a macho show of our seriousness. The new guys had rifles they had never fired. Talk came around to what would happen tomorrow, opening day, and all, especially my buddy, were taken aback when I announced I would hunt alone.

The first days were stumbling ones for us all. We had not scouted the terrain. I knew only barely what "scouting" meant. Fatalistically I accepted that the hunt would be a crap-shoot. Only blind luck would let us even see a deer. We drifted back to the cabin tired that evening, having heard only distant shooting. We drank beer and ate more macaroni, tried to play cards – which I declined, probably to show I was a true hunter, not some damned "Albuquerque Redcoat" released from domestic prison to drink and raise hell in the woods for a week.

So it went. The stranger pair quit hunting early in the day, tired and I thought bored. My buddy worked harder at it and asked me good questions, ones I couldn't answer. Once, perched high on a rimrock, looking straight down on a brushy canyon floor far below, I watched six deer move up it unaware of my presence. They stopped often to browse, moving just fast enough to stay ahead of what turned out to be the two new guys. Before that pair appeared, I had thought of shooting one buck with visible antlers, but decided it was too risky at that distance. The steep trajectory would be difficult to figure, and I knew not how to get down there afterward. I watched until the deer disappeared, fascinated by the undisturbed behavior of the largest wild animals I'd ever watched. That evening I reported the encounter. The new guys senselessly disputed my tale, tried to argue, both swearing there had not been "a single damn deer" in that canyon. I was affronted by their skeptical denial. I swallowed it for the sake of harmony, but resented the implication that I was bullshitting them.

By then, I had noticed small oak trees scattered among blazing aspens in a grove low down, not far from the valley road. Climbing the rugged mountain held no allure for me, and not telling the others, I began to sit in this oak grove, as if I knew – I didn't – that I would never see a deer in the park-like forest above. I didn't look for droppings or acorns, let alone signs of foraging. I was completely ignorant about deer in any real way.

Back against a tree, comfortable and drowsy in the warm afternoon sun, I nearly missed the small deer – antlers! – descending carefully from behind me toward the road and about to enter a concealing ravine. When the buck went behind a blazing aspen, I raised the rifle, trembling immediately, mind racing: a buck, legal if the antlers were big enough! The deer stayed behind the bright tree. I waited; it had to emerge sometime, but when? Was it already aware of me? The wind had little to tell me in those days. I was schooled in that science only vaguely and anecdotally by Field & Stream magazine. Now I was shaking uncontrollably, had to take my finger off the trigger lest the rifle go off accidentally, then realized I was holding my breath and had to struggle against adrenaline to let it out. *Get hold of yourself!* I ordered myself, ignoring by force of will the frantic urging of a body trying to make me pay attention to a more basic question in those critical seconds: *would I really do this awesome thing?* Bathed in the golden glow of the grove, flashing yellow aspens all around, I hung suspended. Some calm returned though

I trembled still. My arms started hurting from holding the rifle up as time crept. Then the deer emerged, oblivious of me.

I fired and was nearly undone when the thunderous roar and recoil of the heavy rifle split the mellifluous tranquility. The deer went down and did not move again. Overwhelmed, I sat and shook violently, tried when I thought I could to light a cigarette, struck match after match before succeeding. A wisp of something like revulsion swept through me: I did not want to walk over to the deer. Maybe I managed some gesture, felt some twinge of sympathy for the great dead beast, but there was no heartfelt contact, no pat on the neck. Possibly I'd have snorted at such "sentimentality."

But now there was real work to do. I'd read the fish & game regulations: bucks with forked antlers only were legal. At least one fork had to be long enough to "hang a ring on." And now I was staring at the lovely head as if seeing it the first time: a *spike* buck! Illegal! Only one antler even had a fork, and it wouldn't hold a ring. This was a predicament, time to think. Instead, I impulsively grabbed the smooth spike, scheming a way out of reporting my novice error to the checking station wardens. I broke the skinny prong by main force after an impressive struggle, finally having to clasp the jelly-like neck between my thighs to get leverage. I threw the antler-tip away, anxiety surging as I discarded truth. I might face charges, a stiff fine, and feared having to face the captain who'd made my rifle possible. But leaving the animal to rot in the woods, as many do in similar situations, never occurred to me. I had not yet recognized the simple truth that death means food for many others. I was caught in a single thought: this deer was *mine*. But my wilful sense of "ownership" ebbed as the magnitude of this deed swamped me in a wave of weariness. I sat and stared at the still form for a long time. Then I dragged the carcass downslope, hung it in a tree near the road and gutted it, saving out the liver. When I was done the sun had gone behind the western ridge. The air was cooling rapidly and I shivered, gore-slimy hands aching with cold, hoping my buddies would come with the car. Owner-proud, I would not leave the deer to walk to the cabin, not far away, and so I waited. Eventually at full dark they came, having heard my shot. Under Orion's sardonic gaze we carried the deer to the cabin and hung it again.

We drank beer then, laughing and yakking, me accepting their stream of questions, told and retold the story, relaxing as the cabin warmed up. We ate the liver my buddy fried and we finished with Jack Daniels, satiated and exhausted. The two greenhorns pooh-poohed my worry about the broken antler. With appropriate self-deprecation, I accepted their validation of my feat, ritually covered over with sarcastic male banter. I was happy.

I couldn't have lied to them successfully about the antler, so didn't try. But I was scheming to do so when we brought the deer to the check station. On the way there, silently obsessed with the problem, I tried to concoct a feasible story why or how this obviously healthy buck had happened to "lose" the particular antler that would verify its legal status. I couldn't say the bullet had clipped it off, for it had split like wood; a bullet would have cut it. Besides, the others knew I had fired only one shot.

What possibly saved me was that the two-man crew at the check station was having an easy day. We novices must have presented a comic sight to the wardens: four guys mashed tightly into an old Ford coupe, a deer stuffed into the too-small trunk of the jalopy, its legs and head hanging out, the trunk latch tied to the bumper to keep the carcass from falling out. The two men came out of the lantern-glow of their field tent with flashlights, laughing and talking as Nimrod struggled with panicky nervousness.

Whadda ya got there?
A deer, somebody said.
You shoot it?
No, he did.

The deerslayer suddenly found his voice and owned up, encouraged by the genial mood of the state men.

It's mine, I said, regretting my choice of words. Then I said, *Seen many deer today?*

Well, a few, the older one replied, then burst out laughing, "I guess we did! Tell em, Jake".

This guy comes in – a while back, before sunset, pickup truck – says he's got a deer to check, an' so we walk around back, an' the fust thing I see is shod hooves. I say, "Where's the deer?" – here he laughed hard, had to stop for breath, continuing when he could,

"That's it! Right there!" he says to me, so I look at Marv an' he looks at me an' then Marv says, *Well, just how fast do you think that cowboy had to ride to put these here horseshoes on this here deer?* Laughter all around, but "Jake" wasn't finished,

"Well, whadda ya mean?" the guy says, "This is my deer." *That durn fool done shot a mule, really thought he had him a deer.*

More laughing banter followed, embellishing details about "damfool Albuquerque Redcoats" while we showed our hunting licenses. At a certain point Marv, straightening up in the chill night, said to me,

Well, lessee whatcha got there.

At first it went all right; we manhandled the stiff gray bulk out of the trunk and weighed it with some difficulty. Then Jake knelt at the head, me watching, tense, standing apart.

Okay...looks like a yearling, I'd say – but what's this? He lifted the head by the good antler. In a moment he murmured softly to Marv a few feet away, who came over and knelt on one knee.

Whatcha got? Oh I see. The two men talked inaudibly for awhile. Finally Marv said, looking at me but speaking as if to all of us,

You a GI?
Yeah – from Albuquerque, Sandia...
Alla ya?
Yeah...
Sandia, huh? He knelt beside his partner a little longer.

The interrogation was brief. I didn't have much to say, didn't have to speak the lie I was living, couldn't face the music, couldn't bring myself to tell the truth about the broken antler. The state men rose and looked at me directly, but didn't put their flashlights in my face. They studied me, not pushing the point, knowing full well what had transpired: the circumstantial evidence could not have been plainer.

It's close, said the senior warden softly, to his colleague, then sternly, ominously, to me,

What you gonna do with this animal?
Eat it, I hope...
You hope... You live in barracks?

Yes, I said, too hastily, then inanely, as if it were crucially important,

I got friends who cook – a perfect lie. The other guys were grouped, looking on silently. Marv and Jake seemed to deliberate, or so I thought, standing rigid before them for I knew not how long. Finally:

This shot was near perfect, so I know you got eyes. Maybe next time, if there is a next time, you'll use em a little better...

Yes, sir.

And so they let me off, tagged the deer, let us take it. We wrestled it back into the trunk and piled into the Ford, feeling relief like sweet balm. Those damn wardens had lied – it was no perfect shot and they knew it; they had to have seen and smelt the fermented gut-stink: my tenderfoot knife, or the bullet, or both, had opened paunch or intestine, flooding the cavity with odorous contents. In the car the guys got on me, my buddy accusing me of recklessness:

Why didn' you tell 'em the truth? That was dumb! You coulda got us all in trouble, accomplices, man.

To this charge I had no defense and kept my mouth shut.

The trip back to base was interminable. Cramped and cold in the back of the coupe I slept fitfully, coming awake once to hear my buddy tell another reason we had been able to use the cabin. It turned out that the Top Sergeant didn't hunt any more. Last year up here, he'd gone to bed after an evening of drinking and playing cards, quite drunk, and for some reason woke during the night and felt for his .30-30, loaded, round in the chamber. For some reason he withdrew it from under his bunk and it went off.

WOW!

"*Yeah – shot himself right na ass!* General hilarity. Someone said,

He coulda killed himself!

Naw - was just a flesh wound, not life-threatening. Guess he bled like a stuck hog, though. This detail accelerated our whooping. We all knew about this bad-ass top-kick, except me who'd never even seen the man, but I laughed anyway, making my corny joke about "justice":

Time wounds all heels.

This sergeant was not only ignorant but stupid, and I wondered how in hell he got to be the Top Enlisted Man in the Armed Forces Special Weapons Project. Self-righteously I remembered the famous "Ten Commandments of Gun Safety" my dad made us learn by heart. That kind of dumb accident I would never make – and of course I didn't think of Bud Duvendak.

The grinding trip in the rickety coupe bore in on us after awhile. Laughing and joking tailed off. Morose, wanting a shower badly, I tried not to think about the morrow. I still had to face that game warden's question squarely: *What indeed was I going to do with this big critter?*

Deer Hunting

I don't know what happened to it. What I remember is blurry, a blustery cold parking lot on a Sunday morning, the deer being taken apart with dull knives and a hacksaw on the hood of a station wagon by older guys, non-coms I had never seen before, with me glumly responding to chaotic dumb questions I couldn't or wouldn't answer, walking away soon as I could...

Years afterward, on a grimly sleepless night of wrestling with my nuclear incubus, looking elsewhere than into myself, I maundered over the trivial notion that I had been let off the hook by those wardens in patriotic deference, theirs, to the nuclear enterprise. New Mexico *was* atomic weapons, perhaps more than Nevada. What else could it mean, the way Marv noted our duty station: "Sandia, huh?" We were treated indulgently because of the uniform, perhaps even by our association with nuclear military might. Or was my thinking already warped by guilt born of that macabre thrall? Was I still unconsciously walking the insane way of "élite soldier, atomic warrior?"

One angle of the hunt I didn't speculate on. In those days humility was the same as humiliation to me. But maybe, just perhaps in that simpler era the senior warden was merely making allowance for a youthful mistake. "It's close," he'd said, studying the strain on my face. Maybe, easier to do than say, it was indeed just sympathetic paternal forbearance to let me go.

XVII
Landslide

In typical American fashion, my buddy and I got "involved with" that old Ford, a coupe so run-down from neglect and age that driving it was a gamble. Once, beneath the Santa Fe railroad overpass downtown, its battery fell through rotting floorboards onto the street, dangling and dragged by its cables, during evening rush hour of course, causing a raucous horn chorus as we frantically struggled to reinstall it and get the damned jalopy out of the angry traffic. The car's owner, a draftee Californian, had long since quit driving it, saying laconically,

That damned thing needs to be put out of its misery. But we continued to use it.

On a trip up Tijeras Canyon east of the city, we accidentally came upon the road to Sandia summit, where we put quarters into a post-mounted Bausch & Lomb optical device and scanned the Rio Grande Valley through dim lenses for the short interval our coins purchased. Exhausting that novelty quickly, we soon left, there being no other amenity at the bald summit. Soon after, we decided to go camping in the forest behind the mountain. With blankets and canteens, on a mild weekend afternoon we found our way to a remote grassy swale between two high wooded hills. Scavenging wood, we made a fire, ate C-rations and talked, drank Jack Daniels, me mostly listening to my buddy's life history. Eventually we slept, embers dying between us.

I knew it had been a good sleep because of the way I awoke: no muscle moved except my eyelids. I was suddenly calmly wide awake. No sun yet. Green grass, tall dark pines, bright blue sky. I faced east. In a moment my eye walked up the grassy slope, and seventy yards above us, backlit by the coming sun, sat a mountain lion on its haunches, calmly looking down on us.

Electrified but motionless, I began making soft hissing sounds to wake my buddy without letting the cat know.

Wake up, but don't move, I said when he moved slightly.

Don't move – be real quiet.

What's up?

If you roll over quietly and look, you'll see a mountain lion looking at us.

No shit! he yelled and whipped off his blanket, grabbed under pillowed clothes and came up with his pistol.

At this commotion, the big cat calmly rose, turned about face and walked unhurriedly over the crown out of sight, the long tail twitching once. And then, unbelievably, clad only in BVDs, my buddy tore off upslope and over the crest, gun in hand, with me yelling after him

No! No! – don't shoot him you idiot! – imagining a weird scenario, the big cat turning on his pursuer with bloody results. But it was not to be. There were no shots. My buddy caught not a glimpse of the animal. After a minute or two he ambled back, snappish at being called an idiot and pooh-poohing any notion of danger in his action.

No! I said, *that was stupid!*

I didn' really want to kill him.

Then why'd you take the gun? A .22 is too small for a job like that, even if you did want to shoot it – you mighta really pissed him off if you nicked him, got in real trouble.

Later, after more arguing, with apples for breakfast and resisting going back to Sandia, we found ourselves at the summit again, dawdling half-heartedly.

Landslide

Is this all there is?

We stepped to the vertiginous rounded edge of the scarp, looked down almost vertically upon leafy cottonwoods far below. One of us skipped a stone over the edge. It gathered rattling speed and disappeared. Many seconds later we heard hollow reports and rumbling as of distant thunder, but saw nothing. Suddenly excited, I loosened a rock the size of a melon and flung it over. This time, after dead seconds of free-fall, there came a spreading roar punctuated with sharp reports. Treetops way down were seen to wave violently, the event lasting many seconds. Heaven may have helped anyone hiking below, though birds and animals were on their own. I suddenly realized what I had done and felt nakedly visible on the bare rock. We left hastily – there was only one road to the summit, easily blocked, and I imagined cops already on their way.

If that were the extent of our spontaneous mayhem... But of course, each of us abetting the other, perhaps conspiring over this new sippin' whiskey, this pair came back again, another day. The chronology is confused but irrelevant in any case – time has no meaning in dreamtime, as Aristotle knew and we have forgotten, it could have been a fortnight later. The old Ford coupe was dying its lingering death, so deteriorated it barely ran. Its owner wanted only to be rid of it – it would take real money to rehabilitate it. Forget restoring it – only a rich screwball could get interested in that – and so perhaps notions of merciful 'euthanasia', stimulated by the finality of its owner's diagnosis, kept us pushing the jalopy up certain steep grades, though it was in gear with the engine running. A prosecutor might call "dedicated" the sweaty exertion by which we achieved the summit with the old junker.

Good! – nobody around, only the silent broadcast towers surveying the valley. Cautious, we waited, perhaps gathering nerve, making sure no one was around to observe. There was no fence, no guard rail at the cliffhead, probably no longer true. All we had to do was push the rusty carcass over the edge – and so we did, leaning into the pressure of the standing breeze sweeping the naked rock, to enjoy a magnificent visual and auditory spectacle reported back to taut grinning faces completely silent so as not to miss any nuance of a growing and seemingly endless roaring cascade down below: we'd started a true landslide! Flocks of boulders sprayed out in slow arcs like giant balls. Trees exploded with reverberating booms and were bashed aside to a great bonking clamor of replicating echoes like howitzer fire, the uproar expanding to a doomsday crescendo on a widening front as destruction rampaged down the cliff, finally to dissipate grumbling and banging into dissected gulches and arroyos at the foot of the cliff. And after a long while billows of ochreous dust rolled out and up like bitter fog.

Dumbstruck, high on adrenaline, when we could speak we replayed the event to one another, animated, maybe trembling, telling ourselves we'd done nothing wrong, this was harmless, just a Tom Sawyer prank – asserting without a shred of justification that no human being had been in the way of the cascading torrent. I never bragged about the escapade – impossible to describe anyway: you had to be there. How we two miscreants got back to Sandia was lost in the afterglow of excitement, not to say anxiety. I was moved to watch the Albuquerque newpaper for a few days, nervously hoping, and hoping not, to see a story about our landslide.

XVIII
WSPG

Surprise, surprise! – change was in the air. We weren't going overseas but posted south: I felt profound relief at our not leaving the country. Logan said,

Don' worry, this'll be line duty too, no idea how long it'll last, could be a only month, then overseas. Private soldiers, last to get the word, can only speculate about the whys of military decisions. Sarge hinted that the 14th was chosen for White Sands Proving Grounds because we were the best at what we did and anyway, White Sands was where the action was: guided missile stuff. We were not just line-qualified but a top-of-the-line outfit.

But the news brought unease with it. Cycling through excitement and anxiety, I had a physical sense of a "bed of mud" inside me, shifting, maybe dangerous. I did my best to hide my inner wrangling, but the fact is, Manning and Branch now lurked ever nearby, and when alone I slid into melancholy which lifted as soon as anyone spoke to me. I let no one into my dark and moody realm, especially if they asked,

You OK?

I would reply with a quick grin, "Oh, sure," then set to bad-mouthing the Church or whatever. Eventually I saw on my questioner's face that he had heard it already, so I would clumsily try to join his conversation. Outwardly I was cheerful and compliant at work, which might even pass for enthusiasm with the guys. If they got on me for that, I was ready to justify my behavior, not altogether disingenuously:

I just wanna see what's next, I would say, and deny my volunteerism was brown-nosing, which of course it was. I seldom missed an opportunity to make myself look good, especially if an officer was involved.

Buckin for a stripe, are ya? said Moose with narrowed eyes.

Some Headquarters officer got the idea I was the perfect man to design the new battalion emblem we were eligible to wear on uniform epaulets: a medallion, not a patch – only regiments got patches. Sarge and Red and Moose urged me to give it a try. How did they know I could draw?

Hell, I don' know anything about this stuff, I said. But later I agreed to try, hesitantly, working around an inner hollowness as I spoke, feeling trapped. Conversation among the four of us brought ideas. I admitted I had seen my family "coat-of-arms" once, in an obituary about some unrelated departed Ellis. I had scorned the notion at the time, seeing nothing attractive in "heraldic imagery" beyond the stupidity of "pedigrees." But hunched over our workbench, we came up with a shield design by the end of the day. I drew it out with a pencil, perhaps overnight, whose finished version you have seen by now.

The Colonel was said to have approved the design at once. The little drawing disappeared and I heard nothing for weeks until suddenly the enameled insignia was distributed. The Heraldic Division had added a banner with a motto beneath my shield: *Accensa Lucerna.* My high school Latin could not come up with a translation. Years later an accomplished linguist decided that, given insufficient knowledge of the context, an approximation might be "The lamp is lit" or maybe "The torch is burning." But reflecting darkly on Cold War insanity, I thought my version better approached truth: *The fuse is lit.*

Word got round of my artistic effort, and soon I was poohpoohing praise from the guys. Nonetheless I had a feeling of "my star rising," further contorting my inner turmoil. English is a flexible language, but embodies no way to say yes when no is meant. I had said Yes again: the damned insignia got me deeper into "the battalion community," made me part of the official history of the 14th Ordnance Battalion (Special Weapons Depot). The Exec Officer would not return my sketch, saying,

Oh no, I can't do that – it has to go into the Battalion archive. Sometime after that, maybe because of it, I made Pfc, but didn't make a connection between my first stripe and being "cooperative and willing." I could no longer envision a future as a soldier, but didn't say so.

Before we went to White Sands I made another trip back east where I bragged about the buck I had shot, passed around the traditional snapshot of it, and again hinted darkly and teasingly to my dad about the battalion mission. I stayed but a short time, found little of interest in my home town, holding tenaciously to the feeling I had no home anymore. Mom was now working again, gone all day; my siblings were nearly strangers. I felt an outsider, here but not really here, except for Grandma. In her seventies, her hands were again full dealing with the youngest kids. Mom was strangely working for the Navy Department. Grandma wondered aloud when I would come home for good, wishing plaintively I would come back at Christmas. I shook my head No, thinking *I wouldn't if I could*, and kept silent at her wistful remark, full of a mix of pity and sorrow I could not summon for my parents. This mournful sighing old woman – "elder" was not in my lexicon then – hoped as long as I knew her that I would find my "true vocation" in The Church. She spoke always of me as her first grandchild. I resented my meaningless natal primacy, slowly coming to see how it tied me to a completely illusory sense of overweening entitlement – "fame, riches, glory" – good grief! Primogeniture was a curse I always resisted verbally when it surfaced verbally – and yet I often acted in keeping with it.

At the door when I was leaving, Grandma pressured me with simple farm-girl generosity into accepting some ripe plums from the driveway trees, which I put into my duffle bag, right on top. My thanks to her were almost genuine. The plums were in a paper bag – that was long before gushing oil wells began to spray thermoplastic membranes into every corner of the land. Later, hungry, I remembered the fruit during the train layover in Chicago – no fast-food franchises then – how I cursed on discovering that the damned plums had fermented, and not sweetly. When I opened the duffel bag they released their sour country essence and a mushroom cloud of fruit flies. The juice had soaked the top layers of not uniforms but precious civvies – bluejeans and short-sleeved shirts.

Madness encompassed as well the circumstances of that spur-of-the-moment trip to Virginia: Earl, a Headquarters Pfc who owned a brand new green-and-gold Hudson Hornet, was planning to go east and sought riders: free, non-stop, just for the company, one way only. I contacted him, then applied for and got leave time to jibe with Earl's departure date. I wondered why strange looks from the guys when I spoke about the forthcoming trip. I had known nothing of the rumors about Earl, so Red told me that one of the brass had asked him whether Earl had "tried anything" after an assignment together on some detail or other.

Whaddya mean? I said.
Well, c'mon guy – you're not dumb.
I don't get it...
He's a swish – a nice guy, but a swish.
How d'you know – he tell you?
Aw, come on man – this from Moose, vehemently, *don' you know beans when the damn bag is open? He's a fuckin pansy, and thass all there is to it.* We had a Mark 6 weapon open

at the time, but Moose's scowl and brutish remark was not a jab to get us back to work. Sarge said nothing.

Deliberately averse to this kind of scuttlebutt, I hadn't heard a thing about this Earl, so I took time to ponder what my mates were saying, unsure whether to believe them or not. The free ride was attractive: the car would be full, we'd go non-stop to Dayton, I could get the &O from there.

Well, far as I'm concerned, this is all rumor, and so what if it's true? He's never done anything to me. They looked at me. Moose fixed me with slitted eyes, then shook his head, once.

So I went east with Earl as planned. We zoomed out of Albuquerque on Route 66, the long trip exhausting because Earl would let nobody else drive his new car. Roaring hours passed, night fell, Earl became a robot, fist grimly locked on the steering wheel hour on hour, yielding only grudgingly to piss calls from his four passengers, mutual strangers all, nobody sleeping for fear Earl would doze off and kill us all.

Some time after I returned to Sandia, I rode downtown with Earl, who chanced to see me waiting for a city bus at the main gate and offered to take me down. Under way and after small talk, Earl entered a line of subtle, tentative questioning. His sentences trailed off, became gambits I wouldn't pick up, obscure references and circumlocutions that seemed to require knowledge that, my back becoming increasingly rigid, I could only guess at. Later I remembered a remark about "Army headshrinkers," but couldn't remember its context or substance. Possibly my body was understanding things I could not articulate. Was this guy trying to find out if I was a "queer" without asking me straight out? Responding equally indirectly, writhing in virginal naïvety, I responded mostly monosyllabically, careful to say nothing that might halt the conversation or offend my driver. I didn't look directly at Earl. In a short time, knowing we would part shortly, nothing to be afraid of here, I recognized feelings of something like "sympathy" in the face of his gingerly indirect talk. Increasingly nervous myself, I felt no aggressive impulse, only wondered where this subtle canvassing was leading. Then, with no answers to his questions, Earl mentioned outright that he was fighting an attempt to discharge him.

Why? I said.

They say I'm an undesirable.

I looked over at him then and saw an expression crafted unsuccessfully to hide strong emotion – fear – saw tiny beads of sweat on his forehead. Silence for a time. I felt massive confusion. It took me a while to understand his announcement as a plea for sympathy. It was a chance for me to speak my thought and ask him,

What does that mean? But of course I already knew. No GI could claim ignorance of the harsh fate of a "queer" discovered. Here was the hellish issue sitting beside me. I sat clenched and speechless. Was this guy telling the truth or just trying to manipulate me? Despite psychic disarrangement that boiled down to fright, I felt an impulse of compassion for the man's plight. But no words came and my tension built, waves of utter helplessness. I sat silent, the elegant Hudson purring on toward downtown. What could I possibly do about this situation? Nothing whatever. After awhile the mounting silence forced me to respond to his stated predicament. I managed, probably feebly, to wish him well, feeling weird and empty inside, the conversation seeming to evaporate as it happened. Just maybe, I said I was glad he was fighting the charge – though I had no idea of the secret process he faced – I didn't even know whether "charges" was the right word, whether he faced court martial, trial or what.

I never saw him again. We had never had an interaction, work or other. Much later I heard he had been discharged under conditions "less than honorable." Nobody in the coffee shop wanted to talk about it. Sensitized to potential consequences for myself should I pursue inquiry, I kept still and let the incident fade. "Homophobia" was perhaps to be found by then in the Oxford English Dictionary, but it was not in regular speech. I would have stoutly denied being bigoted about homosexuality, had anyone accosted me on the issue, but I was already a hypocrite about the issue. I was disturbed by this business for reasons I didn't address, and felt obscure lingering shame at not offering more than timid verbal comfort for this poor bastard who had given me a free ride to Dayton Ohio. Later I was conscious for the first time of being a witness to Army brutality in a new way, for whatever the hell it was worth.

Strange things continued to happen to me, like Moose's invitation to come over on a Friday night for something called "pizza pie." I accepted, why I couldn't say, having little in common with this guy except work and that famous beer party confrontation. I speculated that his invitation might carry an agenda: not likely, but maybe Moose wanted to bury the hatchet. However, when I arrived at the place, in base housing, I almost immediately wanted to leave again. That was out of the question without insulting Moose, so I diffidently entered the company of these married lifers and their spouses – all present were NCOs except Moose. Logan was there, without his wife. Everyone sat around the chrome-and-formica dining table, the unpretentious bungalow cluttered with kitschy bric-a-brac and overstuffed furniture, no kids. I took a proffered beer and praised the pizza. I felt and behaved as an outsider, which I was: young, unmarried and living in barracks. Gamely I tried to join the Friday-night jocularity, but as time passed I found fewer and fewer ways to join the conviviality. Too many corny dirty jokes. I liked a dirty joke as well as the next guy, but this was stale high school stuff, not quite raunchy, juvenile ribaldry flowing freely with the beer. After awhile my face muscles began to hurt from phony smiling at stuff that was not funny. Years later, my involuted mind worming through neurotic pain and starting to address the legitimate and true deprivations of my upbringing, I thought my greatest deficit was conditioned aversion to laughter, which indeed had been almost *de rigeur* when my Dad was in the house. Yet I wasn't totally bereft of humor, appreciating particularly the wry sort – if it came with corned beef and lots of mustard and onions. And unconsciously no doubt, my tobacco habit, keeping irritated bronchi full of mucus, helped physically to keep my laughter from being full and hearty.

At any rate, when I thought sufficient time had passed, I stood up to leave. No one tried to stop me. Moose, well on his way now, thanked me loudly for coming. When I left I was not even faintly high on the one beer I'd put down, being shy about going to the fridge for another one as others did. The wives had grouped off in the kitchen away from their partners, partying on their own, their conversation quite unintelligible until one held up her thumb and forefinger, nearly touching, jabbering and laughing about her mate's effective length. As I went out the door I realized I had not been introduced to, had not even identified Moose's own wife.

As it happened, we were posted temporarily to Holloman Air Force Base, near Alamogordo, east of WSPG. The acronym translated in my mind to "Whistle-pig." During the trip down there in Logan's car, not needed as a convoy driver, I wondered if the groundhogs, once a favorite target back in Virginia, as "whistlepigs," lived in this desert. Halfway there, below Socorro, Sarge pointed out the entrance to Trinity Site: a galvanized cattle gate in an ordinary barbed-wire fence, posted with the usual *No trespassing, US Gov't Property* signs. Immediately I wanted to go down the dirt road, to actually see the place where the first atom bomb had gone off. Sarge wouldn't detour, even though we were well ahead of time. He said,

You don' wanna go down there, prob'ly can't get in, nothin' to look at anyway. I was there once, all you could see was a little sand melted into glass.

His comment intensified my pique, but Logan dedicatedly kept his Dodge at a steady fifty against the vagaries of the road. Sarge was his own "cruise control" in those days before the Interstate Highway System prepared the country for enemy attack. Our speed wavered no more than one or two miles an hour the whole long drive down the Rio Grande valley under the blasting sun. After Trinity Site was behind us, Logan unexpectedly asked if I thought I'd re-up. The question was a seed I buried in mental mud: Was I or was I not a top-of-the-line atomic warrior? My answer was both cagey and casual.

Hell, I don't know, haven't thought about it – it's a long way away.

Holloman was a collection of wooden buildings, a dusty landing strip and a bunch of WWII warplanes, bombers and fighters, prop jobs, strewn across the Tularosa Basin east of White Sands National Monument, our temporary digs until WSPG, tucked up against the San Andres mountains to the west, found proper accomodation for us. Temporary quarters were standard wooden military buildings, decrepit and amazingly dusty. The famous White Sands are light-weight natural gypsum, and every afternoon a noiseless white wall loomed up in the west which eventually swept across Holloman, sometimes blotting out the sun from the eternally cloudless sky. Even with no wind blowing, everything indoors was coated with soft white flour every day, infiltrating even into closed footlockers. It was impossible to keep anything clean, but that didn't matter since we seemed to have escaped formal military ritual and inspections, as well as any opportunity to wear "my" new scarlet-and-gold insignia, not allowed on fatigues. The brass were quartered elsewhere, and we had little work to do – another holding pattern, hurry up and wait. What passed for a PX at Holloman had only three-point-two beer – a grim outpost indeed.

Missile work soon made itself evident from afar, with the aged aircraft: B-17 *Flying Fortresses* were grotesquely misnamed "mother ships." The old *Wildcats* and *Hellcats* were more appropriately called "target drones" – stingless males making no honey and never had. On a mission a B-17 approached from the south where a drone sat warming up for take-off, no pilot at the controls. At a certain point the "mother ship" took radio command from the ground and flew the drone into the air, an eerie sight, no helmeted head in the cockpit. Both planes flew up-range where the drone became a target for a missile test which destroyed the junker if the weapon worked. We might hear a distant boom. If not, the drone used up its fuel and went down, or was perhaps crashed by the B-17 inside the hundred-by-forty mile area of the missile range, two and a half million acres of land stretching north beyond Trinity Site, seized by eminent domain from local ranchers and farmers. The notion of "theft" occurred to me when I heard this, and later became a blunt, accusatory fact in my mind. That judgement might have evaporated had I known of compensation paid in government land-takings. I wondered in my thoughtless way about the people dispossessed; likely there weren't many, and anyway this desert seemed like a true wasteland, not good for much else.

XIX
Playtime

A curious change, almost a conversion, seemed to come over me, a leavening of my shilly-shallying after we settled at White Sands. I showed active enthusiasm both on the job and off. It stemmed directly from our surroundings, the bleak wild grandeur of the Chihuahuan desert. The stark upright fangs of the San Andres range, almost in our backyard, were balanced by a great sweeping slope of mesquite scrub overarched by clear air and blazing sun, hotter than hell at noon even in February, and best of all, a silence I remembered visually as 'beige and blue tranquility,' a dry and bland impersonal calm that could mesmerize me in still moments. Our cantonment on the sandy slope was an urban / industrial sprawl, forever blighted. Battalion quarters were at its northern edge. All I had to do was walk out the north door of the barracks a few rods and descend onto desert floor, stippled with waist-high mounds of thorny mesquite catching sand ever eager to move. It was full of streaking lizards and sudden jackrabbits jumping high in the air to look back as they raced away, keeping airborne track of their pursuer.

But there was excitement of another kind as well. At any moment of the day there might be a booming roar and another rocket zoomed away from five or seven miles out in the basin. Some left the pad so fast I couldn't visualize them. Others rose on stately pillars of fire and billowing smoke, taking many seconds to bend out of sight uprange. Having picked up accessory clues – extra traffic going out to the pads – that a launch was likely on a given day, I discovered that the roof of our new work building, five miles out there, was a good place to wait, hot of course, but elevated enough for an unobstructed view. Sometimes several of us would wait on top for a prospective launch. But the brass soon learned our trick and padlocked the trapdoor. We agitated to go and sit in the bleachers for some of the countdowns:

Hell, we're workin on 'em, why can't we get to see the results? But the answer came back,

You have no connection with what's going on over there. And there's work to do here. But we did have a connection to the launches, witnessing them from afar, and so we grumbled, without success.

Behind our compound was the test track where the famous Colonel Stapp regularly strapped himself onto a rocket sled, touched it off and went zooming down the track into such smashing halts I could not understand how the man survived.[9] Colonel Stapp survived this physically torturing barrage of decelerations and was said to be alive and well at the end of the millennium...

Over at the launch site, Nike anti-aircraft missiles left with thunderous roars on huge clouds of white smoke, disappeared in seconds, leaving a finely-tapered white arc hanging in the azure stillness. Later, the Nike II, larger and carrying radar, underwent testing. A story went around about a press photographer who walked in front of the powered-up radar of one. The high-frequency emissions ignited the flashbulbs in his pockets and seriously burned the poor bastard.

Our own work was depot duty, live warheads from Killeen Base, maybe elsewhere. We started work early, rode in six-bys out to our compound, smoking and matches allowed only in a wooden coffee shack set apart from the operations bays. Military reality was represented by a Thermite grenade posted conspicuously atop the file cabinet where our Top Secret documents were kept. Insulated, far from Cold War propaganda, we hooted at the wild-ass notion we'd ever have to touch it off. *In case of surprise enemy attack*, said the brass – as if the US would ever suffer another Pearl Harbor!

We became aware of an occasional flashing surprise roar of a jet fighter very low over our building, and running outside we could sometimes see the now-distant plane release a missile, a small point of fire and wavering black smoke, followed sometimes by a boom as a *Sidewinder* found its target and another drone bit the dust. We soon grew bored with our indoor routine while all this exciting action went on around us, always at a distance. This élite battalion had expected top-of-the-line jobs in our new assignment, not this repetitive humdrum. Morale began to deteriorate. The officers, privileged to drive their own cars to work, had an easy out; they could escape the heat and dust with a trip back to post on "official business," invented or real. We observed this pattern and soon a deck of cards came out in the coffee shack: blackjack, easy to fold if an officer came along unexpectedly. Seeking the meager gratification of old cold coffee one endless afternoon, I thought to tame the acidic brew with evaporated milk. There was no refrigerator. I couldn't get the milk to pour, even though its weight told me it was not empty. I took out my Boy Scout knife and opened the can fully, and when I bent back the lid I recoiled in revulsion: its complete inner surface was a writhing mass of white maggots. All along we had used flyswatters without wondering where the critters came from – and now the life cycle was plain. I took pride in educating my mates about why there were always flies in the coffee shop.

The dispirited mood of A Company filtered up the chain of command, and soon it was made known that three-day passes were readily available. Guys began weekend treks to the bar-brothels of Juarez in search of "R&R," leaving the weekend barracks mostly to me. Spirits – specifically mine – rose a bit; good dining hall food, real beer and plenty of free time worked a palliative magic on me.

I began to walk evenings in the cool of the desert with my pistol.

By now we had seen and laughed uproariously at the Technicolor film of a German V-2 rocket blowing up on the launch pad, and a Vanguard rocket similarly. One missile I came to admire: a "pure research" rocket called the *Aerobee*, usually launched toward the end of day. It was a white gleaming needle that accelerated smoothly and steadily, ascending almost majestically on a brilliant pinpoint of smokeless light. Fascinatedly I watched them out of sight and wondered where they came down if they rose truly vertically as it seemed; perhaps they were lowered with onboard parachutes. I thought them beautiful because non-military – almost. I wondered if the Aerobee was the work of Werner von Braun, designer of the V-2s that had pummeled and killed Londoners only a few years ago.

The days got hotter. Work hours changed: out to the compound early, coffee break abbreviated, a brief lunch, then off duty as the desert heat reached its peak. Always an early riser, life felt good to me those cool mornings. We now had our own battalion cooks, who treated us as if we were in fact élite troops.

Joshing with Moose on a hot afternoon, I succumbed to a spontaneous quirky playfulness, saying to my erstwhile enemy that I could make my whole body so rigid that he could pick me up like a plank. Moose was skeptical, but he tried it, and sure enough, with every long muscle in my body clenched in isomorphic contraction, I maintained rigidity. Then I thought it would be fun for Moose to carry me on his shoulder, which this man-mountain easily did, down the hall and out into the courtyard where others could witness the feat. I felt my stiff corpus flex like a plank as the big man strode into the blinding midday glare. Moose was supposed to tell anyone we met,

Haill, Ah don' know what happened to 'im – he's been this way for awhile.

It worked – Mister Ford, grave alarm on his face, emerged from the office and walked rapidly toward us across the hot brown dirt, saying loudly,

What happened? Tell me! At which Moose gently laid his stiff burden down, and I burst into laughter, embarassing Warrant Officer Ford, who tried to pretend he'd known it was a joke all along – but I knew we had *had* this arrogant officious crew chief, who walked away sourly, shaking his head, saying

You guys...you're too much.

Later, giddy with my tomfoolery, I felt good, like when I had shown off before my classmates that ambidexterous handwriting japery on the blackboard. Sister Placida's cold words came back to me, stirring old anxiety over her ominous prophecy. The next day, pleasurably sore from my athletic hypertonus, feeling vaguely sheepish at this inanity, I didn't notice that the "plank trick" marked a return to comradery with Moose, months after that beer party mess.

Without anyone telling us directly, A Company came to realize that some of the warheads we were working on were for rockets, not bombs. They were the same Mark 6 devices, dummy warheads again, and we were "gofers" in the service of civilian engineers who were mating Mark 6s to the Corporal missile, an Army weapon guided by a primitive gyroscopic navigation system. Thus, probably to boost *esprit de corps*, we were allowed to witness the launch of a Corporal.

In hot bleachers many yards from the erect olive-drab missile, we sat sweating behind a group of fat pink-skinned engineers making sarcastic jokes about what was going to happen, re-telling the tale of the Corporal – "no live warhead, thank God!" – that had buried itself in a Juarez graveyard and cost Uncle Sam greatly to assuage injured Mexican feelings.

But you can be damn sure greaser politicians got most of it.

We sweated and sat, waiting for the countdown, "watching for the little guy with the match to run out and light it off," as Red put it. Ignition came unannounced, a burst of flame and dust and a great roar; the missile lifted slowly at first, then faster, and soon we were looking nearly straight up. Suddenly we collectively realized we were bent over backwards: the damned thing was repeating the Juarez trip, heading south instead of uprange, and at that moment the Launch Officer pushed a button and dumped the missile's liquid fuel, causing the engineers to abandon the bleachers with shouts of angry derision to run frantically for the parking lot. For this prototypic beast was fueled with "red fuming nitric acid" – an unfurling and descending cloud, a beautiful red waning to orange then brownish yellow, an intensely corrosive vapor that would eat any paint job. The aborted missile landed hundreds of yards south of us with a boom. It was explained that the guidance system had gotten "180 degrees out of phase."

No shit! said Red, *fuckin Army, can't even tell north from south.* At least it worked better than the famous Vanguard, called the "Civil Servant" because *"you couldn't fire it."* Not one of those was ever successfully launched after multiple efforts costing millions. Then some genius military or civilian got the idea of using us in "torture tests" of Mark 6 warheads installed in controlled-climate chambers. It was good duty, almost. We made evening and night rounds to a huge, hangarlike building that roared with heating and cooling machinery. We climbed into chambers of tropical humidity or arctic frigidity to check batteries and cone insertion and other functions of the warhead mechanism, or to reattach a thermocouple whose duct tape came unstuck. We logged notes on temperature, humidity, the hour, all this several times during the night. For that we got "light duty" the following day. I overheard a civilian engineer wonder, referring to the primitive guidance system of the Corporal, when the

Army was going to stop *"throwing all this fuckin money down this rathole."* Laughing harshly, he continued, *"not that I mind it a bit – it's paying the liquor bills."* I enjoyed the rewards of this duty, the break in routine, the novelty, but came to avoid the engineers if I could. They were a cynical and sarcastic lot every one, treating us GIs with stiff detachment that felt like disdain to me. I was aware I was doing work they were getting paid for. Sarge offered me no relief when I bitched about "sorry-ass engineers," saying

They've always been that way. You suck the public teat long enough, makes you mean, even to your own grandmother. Jus' do your job an' don' worry bout them.

But "worry" I did, finding their cynicism almost – I hated to use that word – *unpatriotic* – and to boot, they got huge salaries for their nasty attitude.

In treks in the desert, without purpose or object, I wandered past the warning signs – *Danger! Hazardous Area!* – among torn remnants of experiments, jagged and twisted aluminum shards, braids of colored wire bizarrely entangled in thorn scrub, even small rockets stuck at angles into the sand like darts – dismal military wreckage. But I learned to ignore it, blotted it out and began to feel something else in the desert. There was an impalpable but gratifying aura about the desiccated scrub. Something endured beneath all the junk. A question seemed to hang, waiting to be solved. I was unaware of projecting my turmoil onto the military desolation I wandered through. Sarge had again queried me, still gently, about reënlisting, and again I put off a candid response. I truly hadn't thought about it, but realized that the question was now a "worry" I had to live with.

The desert mystery, the tenuous scraps of living stuff, the invisible biota of daylight desert became a mental itch. I had no names for the rarely-seen critters or the cacti, the sparse grasses or scraggy shrubs. But this harsh and sere landscape *meant* something, I was sure. Squatting on my heels at random, letting my eyes rest on a thorn-twig or the far mountains where Cloudcroft was, turning over that enigmatic name in my mind – "Indian country" up there – a slow repose might come over me, like in the woods back home. But this was different. I didn't have to think about anything, as if an empty mind defined freedom. I carried but did not shoot my pistol, somewhat fearful that its report might bring a jeepful of MPs. The warning signs did not distinctly forbid trespassing, and I knew I would have to go some distance north run afoul of unexploded ordnance.

Two thirds through my enlistment. I had made no enduring friendships, not even with the hunting buddy left behind at Sandia, who in any case would soon be released to real life. We had done a lot together – a trip to Vegas, that landslide, that mountain lion – but practically the sole thing we agreed on in all our beer-drinking lolly-gagging was the quality of Jack Daniels Sour Mash Bourbon. We would probably never see each other again, and only decades later, when finally my loner mind began to circle near the vicinity of heart matters, could I confess there had been a shred of intention to *let the guy go* when we debarked for White Sands. Life was that way: born alone we are, and free. Staying away from Jefferson's entangling alliances was a man's task.

Dreamtime encompasses much of what I went through: taking that one step forward, that drill sergeant smiling a suddenly wicked grin as he told us "how it was going to be from now on." Jumbled non-sequential memories refusing to disappear into time, had sintered into intricate amorphous fusion, the swirl of events commingling, cause and effect reversing, and reversing again, memories flashing and winking like the Aurora Borealis I had never seen. I thought I was insane, mad, but who cared? For my dreamtime – I only named it thus years later – was a whole, an entirety, one to which "totality" was irrelevant. That recruiter, Gaffney, Philadelphia, the terrible pair Branch and Manning, Eberhard the medic, that temporary machine gun team.

Names gone willy-nilly, the GI Bill, everything is all there, that Roman-candling paratrooper and fragrant hush puppies, an enduring, shifting, ever-changing matrix of inner galaxies, a limitless mass thronged not solely or even principally by human beings. Feelings too, vast interior sorenesses, stunning shocks and depthless yearnings, the musty myth of love never had, snippets of victory, sweet idylls, tinges of real peace which must come – if only I hung on long enough.

These interludes, whether or not on a desert walkabout, brief in the context of battalion dullness, might lead back to old fears of epilepsy I thought I had met head on, thought I had dissolved. Fear was a force I had to reckon with, shown by my sudden jangling hypervigilance aroused by Logan's interest in my putative re-upping.

Why do you ask? I wanted to say but didn't. After awhile I grasped that if I said No to Sarge, consequences would follow, though I didn't know what they might be. But yes, I did very much want promotion to Corporal; hence I thought it good to play my cards close to my vest. Maybe diligence and keeping my nose clean might work in my favor. I had not decided yet and was determined to make my decision without help. I needn't be afraid of Logan, I could handle that problem, which wasn't even a problem. It was not in the universe of my imagination to recognize this fear as *sui generis*, a pattern deeply rooted in accumulating mental mud, kept ever slippery by a tireless and clever ego. The narcissistic orientation, of course, functions equally toward future and past, as if with eyes 180 degrees apart. If my "self" ever danced in the now, it did so in split fashion, scanning the past or scheming the future; or fixed monomaniacally on something always outside myself, steering slickly away from the here and now.

XX
The Pressure is On

Honest John was mounted on a slanting I-beam track atop a six-by, and flew at whatever compass azimuth its driver happened to park at. The rocket, shaped like a huge sharp-pointed mortar round, was therefore ballistic, like a Scud.[10] Arrowlike, its range was adjustable by elevation above the horizontal. It could fly far, they never told us how far. It carried a Mark 6 nuclear warhead, making it a *tactical short range weapon.* Crews from A company, specialists in the Mark 6, were now *ordered* to witness a test firing. Again we found ourselves in bleachers on a hot windy day, sweating, sand in our eyes, me wondering if the weight of the missile rendered its flight immune to crosswind drift. Honest John was fired from a tent or a truck-bed or dugout, connected by cable to a panel like a switchboard. The cable ran out and plugged into the rocket body with an 88-pin connector. In the center of this plug was an explosive charge, and Honest John's last electrical task on launch was to fire that charge and blow plug and cable away from the departing rocket.

A recent firing with a dummy warhead had nevertheless come close to doing in its Launch Officer. Excess cable was coiled near the man's seat. He threw the switch and Honest John promptly took off, but failed to disconnect its "umbilical cord," which writhed and thrashed around like giant snake in the little shack near the launch vehicle. Everything rushed after Honest John with furious speed, including the officer's chair, but fortunately spared his badly-shaken self.

Thus with avid, cynical and voyeurist interest we awaited countdown – off to one side, not behind the big rocket with its fiery rooster-tail. In due course, without a countdown, while Red was again joking about "the little guy with the match," Honest John split our eardrums and blasted off with an enormous flame, kicking up a huge cloud of sand and dust. It roared and soared hundreds of yards, then seemed to hesitate as if saying *Aw shit!* and dropped heavily to the ground where, its fuel far from used up, it proceeded to leap crazily and frog-hop across the desert until exploding with a great boom: the remaining fuel detonating. That was it, all over in less than a minute, unless we count sarcastic whooping in the bleachers.

Lessons were learned of course, that's what tests were for: "Keep that excess cable looped away from Fire Control." As I listened to the wrap-up, however, I was concentrating on Honest John as a tactical, *short range* weapon, another nuclear artillery piece. There was also inordinate danger from the so-called "solid fuel," far from safe or reliable, touchy as hell in fact, maybe more so than TNT and just as unpredictable, with great destructive power.

If dreamtime is truth, which it is, and if truth be more powerful than TNT, which it is, then one must traffic gingerly with it: fact, fancy, ignorance, speculation, fabrication; all these inhere in dreamtime. But traffic with it we must:

Here I am in my father's old car that summer of '55, driving west in a Hudson Commodore, a '47 model, a top of the line sedan with doors that closed like a bank vault. This thoroughly astonishing gift from the old man necessitated ending my leave early, because to cross the whole country in four days meant hustling to avoid arriving AWOL. Suddenly aware that I had less than a year remaining, I told Grandma with a big smile,

I'll be back before you know I've been gone.

At goodby time my Dad said, *My advice to you is, if that thing breaks down in the middle of Kansas, leave it there and buy a bus ticket.*

But once under way, no longer a greenhorn driver, conscious of the need to press on, I nonetheless stayed too long with an aeronautical engineer uncle who mentioned his work on a Top Secret project at Wright-Patterson Air Force base: nothing less than the mad dream, now-forgotten,[11] of powering airplanes with nuclear reactors. I was dumbfounded by his sketchy revelation, but of course, without knowledge of either engineering or nuclear physics, I still understood at first hand the great weight of plutonium, and of the lead shielding necessary to protect a crew from radiation.

It must be based on the B-36, I ventured, remembering the behemoth that had plagued so many evenings at Sandia.

No no no – that's plane's obsolete. This is completely new – I can't tell you much more than that. I gave brash country-boy skepticism to my uncle, but he assured me that Air Force engineers knew exactly what they were doing.

I continued westward, the car operating OK, needing a quart of oil now and then, and the only incident came in St. Joseph Missouri. Coasting to a stop at a red light, I pressed the brake pedal and nothing happened. The heavy car rolled straight through the intersection. Fortunately no one was crossing on the green. Panicked, I stopped, using first gear, ignition off. Opening the hood, I had no idea what to do. A passerby informed me that the Hudson needed brake fluid, maybe more than that, and directed me to a nearby garage. A drink of brake fluid seemed to take care of the problem. The incident cost little, luck in my favor, for I had to husband my few dollars for fuel. This American luxury car was no fuel miser.

Wishful thinking on the hypnotic Great Plains gave way to implacable fact: I would not make it to White Sands on time.

The rest of the trip I worried about being AWOL. True to my pattern, worry is what I mainly did, pushing on urgently, cramped foreboding possibly keeping me awake. The endless miles unrolled in a flat green haze of hot wind and thirst and suspended time. I saw myself as an ant, found no comfort in learning what real patience is, absorbing with every cell what I was experiencing, the breadth of this immense country, stressed but not admitting the stress, of inadequate rest and food I actually had to pay for, overawed by the unending vast emptiness flowing placidly by, so radically different to perception from that TWA flight to Albuquerque. Probably I found at some point I couldn't continue without a break. Likely I stopped and dozed behind the wheel in fitful sweaty naps, "company punishment" hanging over me, real sleep impossible in the heavy torpid humidity of late summer on the Great Plains.

Not only would I arrive late, it was sure to be noticed because it would be a work day, Monday. Logan would wonder where I was, might even ask new First Sergeant Wicket if he had heard from me. This thought stirred something close to panic. I calmed down after awhile – the new top kick was a laid-back sort, already known as Gene, a mild lifer well along in a thirty year career. But new top kick notwithstanding, I had no excuse, no way to fake anything, just had to face the music and take the heat. It never crossed my mind to telephone: what to say? Heavy old Rocincante plodded on west, Route 66, creeping closer, forever. Hours more, below Albuquerque down the long road south through Truth or Consequences and Socorro, past Trinity Site, working hard to avoid road hypnosis in dry heat and blinding sun. I had no canteen. I was no "softie," and in truth, lost and floating in hazy anxiety of my own making, I didn't perceive my dehydration.

Finally, Alamogordo and Holloman were behind me. Route 17 to Las Cruces crossed the Tularosa Basin and White Sands. When a launch is scheduled traffic is halted at the boundaries of the range and released after the shot. Sweaty-palmed, I was thus delayed for itching minutes, but saw no missile – sometimes launches were cancelled – and it was midday when I turned onto the Post road, cotton-mouthed, hyper-alert, just a couple more miles south, wondering if the MPs at the gate would ask for my papers, bracing myself for anything that might happen, which indeed was the case:

With perfect timing as if precisely scheduled for my arrival, there was a stupendous detonation on post. A huge cloud of smoke mushroomed up several seconds before the massive booming roar reverberated off the San Andres, whitely silhouetting the gatehouse just as I rolled up to it, its MP occupants tumbling out of the little kiosk to stare stunned at the distant cataclysm, then running for their jeep. The single remaining guard impatiently waved this shocked exhausted AWOL Pfc on, amid the rising wails of emergency vehicles headed for the site, which I could see was the Nike test stand. Up against a rock wall, solid fuel rocket motors were anchored vertically to bedrock and fired to measure their thrust. Something really bad had happened, but I took the first gravel street right, went up the hill and whipped into the A Company parking lot, got out of the car, not a soul around, walked rapidly to the Headquarters office, meeting no one and hurried to the sign-in book. I signed myself in as of *the day before*, then quickly got luggage and my ditty bag from the car and installed myself in the barracks, put on fatigues and boots and went back to the office to meet First Sergeant Wicket.

What's happened?

Oh, howdy – it's in the Nike area – haven' seen ya for awhile – you been on leave?

Yeah.

Wicket, nobody's fool, questioned me in the same congenial tone he used with everyone, speaking words that showed no suspicion, thus letting me feel a slight breathless thrill as I assured him I had been back since yesterday. Such was the foxy agility of my opportunism that later I felt it really didn't matter how careless I was, I didn't even have to be careful: I was lucky, period. The guys in the barracks and tolerant old Logan seemed to know of my *de facto* AWOL but said nothing, and neither did the brass; that was what counted. Life as nuclear missile warrior resumed.

You didn't miss nuthin, said Red, *at least nuthin important.* The explosion that saved me completely disappeared two engineers, blood, muscle and bone, "vaporized" as Red put it. And there was more, it turned out a few days later: an MP guard at our work compound had gone nuts and tried to machine gun the B Company commander, a martinet captain widely known for his disciplinary cruelty. Assigned in pairs, the guard's buddy had wrested the loaded grease gun from the man; no shots fired.

Shortly my "luck" was tested again, though I wouldn't recognize so for decades: a "Volunteers Wanted" notice on a bulletin board caught my eye. Men were needed to go to Mercury Flats Nevada to take part in "exercises" relating to a coming nuclear test. I quickly asked Logan to forward my name, but Sarge looked at me strangely and said,

Naw – you don' wanna go there, bitterly disappointing me, to miss out on a chance to see one these things actually go off.

Why not? But Sarge said no more. I asked him again:

I'd really like to be in on that. But he merely shook his head and said,

We need you here. It's OK to volunteer; sometimes it's necessary – but not this time. Brash I certainly was, but didn't pursue my crew chief's enigmatic refusal. Perhaps he had heard scuttlebutt he wouldn't share; in any case his veto may have saved me from early death or lifelong sickness.[12]

The new car changed my life immediately of course: a "safe" place to keep the pistol where I could get it any time. We weren't likely to face surprise inspections of our footlockers, but you never knew – this was the Army. The Hudson was also a storage closet, for Jack Daniels or anything of a bootleg nature, which hardly applied to me those halcyon days before "illicit drugs." Now I could drive off post and ramble the desert off duty. One day I noticed a distant bright green spot against low brown hills: oasis. Parking, I trekked a long way across the scrub, in and out of shallow dry washes, avoiding patches of devils's claw and fishhook cactus, eventually closing on the place – farther off than it looked – and at a certain point, crossing barbed wire, I half-saw black objects within the greenleaf cap of the grove. No wind, just heat and blinding glare, utter stillness too real to be spooky. Yet I felt an edgy expectancy, almost suspense as I moved toward the grove, unconsciously adjusting my footfalls to tread lightly, squinting to see into deep pools of black shade beneath the inviting lustrous green of the canopy. Suddenly, great rustling flaps of dry wings made the hair on my neck rise: vultures took to the air, disturbed from midday torpor, carving whooshing arabesques as they fled, the hot air so thin the ragged figures had to flap vigorously. I saw a cow then, bedded down at a distance, recognized the clichéd bovine silhouette. I saw something strange about it and walked toward it wondering. I saw puzzling black spots on the rich Hereford hide. My angle of vision changing subtly with motion, I suddenly saw I was looking through the animal's eyeholes: this critter was dead.

The hide had dried in place, bones all in a jumble inside the hollow hairy shell – dead a long time, no smell at all. Queasy none the less, I backed off, squatted and smoked, lingering long, studying the desiccated form that faithfully preserved the three-dimensional shape of its former owner, dead so long not even one fly buzzed. After awhile I explored the rest of the oasis, an ex-oasis now, my footfalls raising dust puffs that hung in the air behind me. There was a shallow poured-concrete basin full of leaf litter and a windmill tower with its mechanism gone. Many more bones and scraps of hide were scattered around the somnolent grove, no telling how many head. I found myself reluctant to leave and felt somehow "weird" for that. There was nothing to hold me here in this place of stifling air and mass death, yet I felt a baffling strange attraction, even though I was thirsty now. I still don't know why I resisted leaving.

Weeks later I met a local man who showed me how to point-shoot my pistol, "from the hip," and in the course of our conversation learned that the water tank with the dead cows was indeed part of the missile range, land taken by the government in '45, ranchers given thirty days to get their cows off. Such scant notice made it impossible to round up every head in the intricate jumble of dissected brushy foothills. The remaining steers were abandoned to die of thirst, and obediently did. Novice gunslinger in my new straw cowboy hat, I did not miss the bitterness tinging my laconic informant's voice.

Other things were happening at work. I was "volunteered" to paint a sign identifying Headquarters, 14th Ordnance Battalion (Special Weapons Depot), to be mounted on a post in front of the office. It had to incorporate my battalion insignia design. I balked; my response was that of a prima donna. I'd already done my share, the hard part; let somebody else do the detail work. Aloud, I said I was no sign painter, had no idea what to do, even where to begin. My mates countered that nothing I could say would change the fact that I clearly had more skill than they did. All denied any ability to even draw a straight line.

Go down to Quartermaster, said Logan, *get a piece of plywood, two feet by two feet.*

So I painted the sign, grumbling the while, trying to keep my injured ego to myself. But something darker was there too. My mind had shifted. My balking was about more than wounded pride. It resurrected, made real the pervasive shame of my complicity in irredeemable hideousness. I was hip deep in it. Branch and Manning had gotten to me. I could deny all I wanted that my dark inner struggle definitely involved good and evil, denial made stronger by a haunting fear that my complicity had transmogrified into a ghastly "explicity." In my pattern, aware, I nonetheless continued to fend off that feeling, to stuff it, though less and less successfully.

The mechanics of lettering the damned sign gave me great difficulty. I worked hard in resentful silence; immersion in the task was a way to quiet surging inner questions. This sign was just gung-ho boosterism for these yahoos. I wanted no part of it, but it was too late. I finished it with no pride in my work despite praise from the brass, and did not photograph the result when the damned thing was mounted.

But I couldn't stay entangled in self-wrangling for long. I was an élite soldier. I didn't know how truly and madly that was so. By now my bunkmates knew of the revolver. One weekend, no cadre around, I was clowning around with the piece. Slightly tipsy, maybe more, I posed for a snapshot on my bunk with a couple other guys in the frame. In the photo I am pointing the – unloaded! – six-shooter at my head. I sent the snapshot to my mom in a letter reflecting shameful passive-aggressive hostility. Perhaps it survives in the detritus left after her passing, but it seems not. It must have been a provocative letter. A response to it, from her or anyone, would have at least been a response, but none came. In my torment, my parents were convenient psychic targets. My anger at their mad compulsive breeding seemed to expand, to become an awesome vacuity inside me. Bottomless empty hunger for what could never be satisfied was beyond my ability to articulate, therefore allowed only tormenting half-glimpses into my turmoil.

In calm moments I dwelt on the future. My tour of duty would definitely end, meaning decisions to make – but not immediately; *sometime*. Whether to re-up or leave the Army: What would I do if I took discharge and returned to civilian life? College was on my mind, feebly at first and made thinkable by the GI Bill, Public Law 550. I was eligible. Acute awareness of my ignorance dogged me, even in small stuff like not knowing the names of the desert critters around me, a growing itch to satisfy intellectual curiosity. The search impulse is inherently natural in narcissism. Sometimes my mind could escape compulsion to address the world outside itself. History, philosophy, literature – but not art – called me. A more immediate problem would be how to make a living "on the outside." I was fully aware of my service dependency: a bunk and three squares a day, free medical care, clothes, these things had acquired weight, were "not to be sneezed at" as Logan put it. Out of the question to go back to pumping gas for Charlie Barber. But I knew little else and at any rate, with luck in my favor, which it always seemed to be, I thought I would certainly find something. It never occurred to me that making a living on my own required personal attributes I had hardly been exposed to, never mind internalized, qualities above and beyond blind obedience. Initiative, dedication and skills were needed. College seemed to point to a different path from any workaday endeavor I could think of, making it attractive. But anxiety arose when I pondered it: everything I'd ever heard about college seemed to suppose a solid grip on mathematics right off. Rock-bottom competence was required, in algebra, trig, even calculus. I had never even heard of "differential equations."

My mind went stiff at the thought of math.

XXI
Waffling

Wandering slackly in and out of the latticework of routine, I escaped when I could, took to driving over the pass to Las Cruces to drink Jack Daniels by myself in an empty bar for the few days after payday when I had disposable income. Sometimes it was evenings at the post beer garden, staying on after the guys went to chow, or less often a movie, always alone. Locked up in myself, I didn't see that my moods and behavior were being observed. I would have scoffed at the notion of cadre taking care of their men, or if they did, only insofar as manpower scheduling or tracking transfers or expiring tours of duty. A comment from Logan made me perk up:

You seem to like that pistol – you any good with it?

No, not very, but I will be...

There's some guys trying to get up a pistol team, shoot in competition – you be interested in that?

Hell, I don' know, maybe...There's nothin you have to do. Those guys go out every week, practice with .45s. I can tell 'em you'd like to go along and try out.

"Competition" shooting has a different meaning from team sports, all of which I detested and always would. With a gun and paper target, your competition is yourself, nobody else, unless indirectly.

And so I found myself after the heat of the day in a bouncing jeep with an issue .45 and some ammo, headed toward a distant firing range in the foothills. I took to the game immediately. Red tried it for a few weeks, then dropped out, leaving me and one other guy from B Company. We got a jeep from Chavez, weapons and ammo from Kayo and off we went. The older men who initiated us soon quit coming. Maybe they had less need to practice or used a proper firing range, not this barren arroyo littered with shell casings. Stacked ammo crates sufficed to affix our targets, if we had remembered thumbtacks. We stayed until we used up all the ammo. Holding the .45 with an iron grip, I concentrated on the rigorous self-control this game required, striving for total uniformity, tried to will myself into the same mental and physical state for each shot. The repeated hammering soon made the web between thumb and trigger finger sore. A blister appeared. My very intensity, the opposite of one-pointedness – which I knew nothing about – caused the blister. Sore, but persevering and learning, I loosened up and began to put holes in the black of the target.

I was more serious than Caslow, despite his MP training, though he was a better shot than me. One day he suggested we take a grease gun along with the .45s. I'd never fired an automatic weapon and was intrigued: a real machine gun. In a moment of rationalization I thought as a soldier I should know all the weapons in the Battalion TO&E. Kayo was agreeable, so we took one and made much noise that afternoon, used up an entire case of ammo. We made splinters of wooden crates at increasingly closer distances, though the vast majority of our slugs scattered widely, so difficult to control is that cheap ugly alley cleaner. For the first time ever, I met a shooting iron I did not like. I was glad I'd "gotten it out of my system." But I was not turning over a new leaf. On the jeep ride out we often started up jackrabbits, and by taking turns driving, the other one was free to whang away at a jack zig-zagging through the brush – to zero effect but great fun in the trying.

The end toward which we practiced was going to be a blast: the Fourth Army Rifle and Pistol Matches, coming up. We would go to Fort Sill officially, on orders. If we camped out and took turns driving non-stop in one car, we could pocket the cash the Army would supply for rations and lodging. Nobody had recently mentioned re-enlisting, but the seed Logan had planted was germinating. It slowly seeped into my mind that I was being treated extra well to encourage me to re-up. The cooks were open and generous and steak and shrimp appeared often. The dining hall, open for MP shifts around the clock, let us have a snack any time or even a predawn customized breakfast. Three-day passes were to be had for the asking. The cushiness of this life was not aimed specifically at me, I saw, but its consequence was that my moral unease seemed to sequester itself.

The highlight of that summer was a camping trip to the Gila Wilderness with Red and two other guys. One who had been out there would guide us. Amazed by the privilege, we got use of a battalion 4 x 4 from the motor pool, a real Dodge Power Wagon, including jerry cans of fuel. Off we went, lavishly provisioned with a huge food box of T-bone steaks, eggs, milk, baking potatoes, orange juice, other delicacies. We drove out past Silver City, turned north to the trailhead near the Arizona border arriving at sundown. We camped by the truck and ate until we couldn't eat any more and rolled out sleeping bags. In the morning we packed up and set off on a trail into a deep narrow defile filled with lop-sided boulders bigger than automobiles, which required us to jump from rock to rock above roaring whitewater. Someone years before had made a catwalk above the river, now largely gone, but its steel bolts still protruded from stone. At one jumped gap we saw in the black-and-white torrent below an eroded carcass, a mule deer buck wedged into rocks and deadwood. It lay on its back, but mighty antlers on the intact head showed starkly above the dark rushing current. At first glance it looked peacefully asleep, with no discernible cause for its demise. We stared and yakked for awhile and went on.

The pinched mouth of the canyon eventually broadened out. The river was full of trout. *Why hadn't I brought my fishing rod?* We trekked up the dark forested canyon bottom and met a Hereford calf. A strange place for a calf, resting on the forest floor, no mother nearby. Its forelegs were doubled under in normal bovine rest posture. It tried to stand up when we came, but got only its hind legs under it. The front legs would not unfold no matter how forcefully, handling it, we tried to straighten them. Alert for an aggressive mother charging from the brush when the calf bawled at our effort, we finally went on, leaving the critter to whatever fate awaited it: *Mountain lion'll get it,* said our guide, *maybe coyote – but not wolves – they're long gone from here.*

In late morning, sweltering, we came upon a broad, deep pool in the river, sunlit with a natural beach. Sweat-soaked and glad to put down field packs heavy with meat and potatoes and beer, on a sudden impulse we disrobed and threw ourselves yelling into water so cold that I jumped out just as quickly, numb to the core and shaking violently, my groin hurting as if kicked in the balls. I was content to watch the other guys thereafter. Some actually swam, if briefly, in this liquid ice pouring off some mountain somewhere. At one point Red, Minnesota ice fisherman, stood still long enough that numerous foot-long trout, which had disappeared at our first splash, re-materialized to circle round him slowly in the crystal water, studying him, gently nosing up to the novelty of two white hairy pillars new to their pool. Perhaps they were Gila trout, creatures found only in that watershed and beginning their slide toward extinction.

We hiked until late afternoon and camped under huge trees I didn't know, not ponderosa pine in any case. They were too massive to encircle and so tall they had to be really old. Maybe this was true virgin forest. Red said something about being in a cathedral. His odious comparison affronted my hostility to religion, but I managed to keep my mouth shut, taken myself by the silent grandeur of the unspoiled grove. The boulder-filled canyon mouth was too clogged to get these trees out in simpler days before helicopter logging. There was no sign a tree had ever been cut here.

A campfire, Coors beer, potatoes roasted in coals with broiled T-bones, Jack Daniels to finish off with. We unrolled our sleeping bags and lay talking for a while about mountain lions and the calf. Stars emerged, a densely glittering blanket between utterly black treeforms. Silence pressed in and we fell silent with our thoughts – or lack of them, sleep coming stealthily, the unutterable peace of wilderness, carefree, absolute, no warheads, no missiles, no military bullshit.

In early morning, sore hiking muscles notwithstanding, I awoke before anyone else in deep cool predawn gloom, floating in mingled discomfort and a strange and pure aura of soft feelings I couldn't name and didn't need to, wet in the crotch. I lay a long time with the down bag unzipped, and eventually noticed a swish of motion far up in the tops of the trees; it was full bright day up there. The motion resolved into squirrels, more than one, obviously feeding on something, just what I couldn't tell. The trees were evergreen, not hardwoods. When the other guys began to stir I wondered aloud if they might like fresh meat for breakfast, but got no clear answer. I began to shoot at the squirrels anyway, missing and missing and missing. My firing became sextets of measured bangs, each fusillade punctuated by a pause to reload. The critters were so high they seemed not to notice the bullets whizzing by them, which irritated me and made me try harder until finally I had to concede reality. The noise ended when I realized that occasional soft thumps close by were returning spent slugs: I was shooting almost vertically. I had used up nearly a box of ammo and not one bushytail had fallen. The guys ribbed me mercilessly: *What the hell you think you can do at Fort Sill with shootin' like that?*

Came a voice at that point:
Hallo-o-o...
Red answered back,
Hello? A gaunt figure with a rifle was standing at a distance under trees at the mouth of a side canyon. Silence for nearly a minute as this stranger moved toward us.

What's all the shootin' about? the hailer called out, sauntering slowly and deliberately. He was full-bearded, making it hard to tell his age, and wore a wide-brimmed hat, bluejeans, moccasins and had a Winchester cradled in his left arm.

Oh we were just tryin' to get a squirrel or two for breakfast...

With all that shootin? He stood several yards from us, perhaps mindful that this was a four-on-one situation. His eyes, hard to see under his hat brim, narrowed when he spotted my pistol. More terse questions from him with voluble responses. He studied our answers, day now coming on full with sunshine and bird calls. He took his time and set the tone, using the silences. He lived nearby, he said after awhile. He liked it here because it was peaceful "and thought a damn war was startin' down here." Contempt tinged his comment – *"Hell, if you wanted squirrels to eat you should've asked me."* He had a rifle and it would be no trick at all. But we had had no idea anyone was even around. Our questions to him he turned aside or left unanswered.

How long you staying? he asked finally. The query seemed inflected like an assertion. By then we were responding as if we were trespassers, regardless that this was a federal wilderness open to all and shooting game for subsistence was legal.

Dreamtime images lurked in my mind. I felt a sense of identification with this guy despite the mild tension of these circumstances. I remembered old fantasies from before I escaped home.

I thought I saw some version of myself in him. Answering his question without consulting each other, we decided we would be leaving today. Someone said so. The bearded stranger – hermit? fugitive? outlaw? – as if satisfied he had done what he had come for, turned on his heel and noiselessly returned whence he had come without another word. I was of course supremely embarassed at my noise-making and quickly empathized with his complaint. But his complaint rankled too. This wild canyon was public domain. I fumbled with these conflicted feelings but soon smothered them. This hermit, if that's what he was, had dissolved my fantasy of walking a wilderness where no man had ever walked. Failure to bring down at least one squirrel was humiliating. Shortly I realized the guys had really been talking about the racket as much as my poor aim. I had totally destroyed the peace of this canyon, the nearest I had ever come to "primal experience." But I sloughed it off, drowned in morose dejection: these fuckin guys couldn't care less about living off the land, even if only by roasting a token squirrel.

We wended quietly back down the canyon. No trout were seen; nobody mentioned another dip in the icy pool. I had really fucked up, but understood just how only years later; drifting in dreamtime, I wait for a fugitive image of that solitary wraithlike recluse to float up. I have to step carefully around fictive temptation. No use trying to flesh out an image blurry with decades. I retain for sure only the beard, the wide hat and moccasins – and the cradled .30-30. I hear birdsong faintly; shafts of sunlight slant overhead as if portending the descent of some god. Now of course, living next to a big woods, with animals visiting me more than the people I have come to love, I sink into the unbearable richness of survival. I still feel the numinous aura of that wild Gila River canyon, dreamtime itself, and sense a creative solution, fumbling at double binds without number in a life always on the margin.

"Depression" was an infrequent word in those days. One was "moody" or had "gotten up on the wrong side of the bed" or "needed a piece of ass." Even so, the "science" of psychology still struggles today with adolescent Cartesian bias. No one asked me if I was depressed. They noticed without comment as I spent longer and longer evenings at the beer garden, or stared quizzically when I tried with obviously limp conviction to be my "cheerful self." I was still banging away with the .45 though, fifty rounds a week, and sleeping much when off duty.

Out of the blue in July I was promoted to Corporal, briefly raising my spirits. But Logan said,

Don' bother to sew on stripes – they're changing things around.

I disregarded him and stitched on the double chevron with appropriate self-deprecation. I was proud to have "line" rank as a non-commissioned officer, which however lasted but nine days. More new orders came distinguishing me as a "Specialist Fourth Class," with the same pay and benefits, but no longer "qualified" for command responsibility. I was a technician. Only. New ugly sleeve patches replaced the chevron. Nevertheless I was put on the duty roster for "Charge of Quarters" detail. CQ – what a joke, tying up the whole weekend sitting behind the First Sergeant's desk, feet propped on the slide-out tray, dozing in desert heat and silence. The battalion phone never rang evenings or weekends, and it was an insult to be "in charge of" the latrine duty crew. Two memories from CQ remain: late one night, I watched a mouse smaller than a silver dollar quietly play around the base of a barrel cactus that stood outside the open office door. It seemed to be eating tiny seeds or perhaps small insects felled by the night light directly above it. Suddenly the tiny rodent clenched for a split second then leaped. Where it left in the nick of time a giant black spider landed, clearly intent on the critter's life. It was much bigger than the mouse, and soon retreated into darkness, leaving me staring intently. I wished the

Atomic Weapons Mechanical Assembler - 431.10

Assembles, modifies, and performs surveillance of atomic weapons and associated equipment. Installs, tests and adjusts mechanical components using mechanics common and power tools. Prepares atomic weapons for nuclear arming. Tests electrical length of cables using cable tester. Assists in FAT test to determine acceptability of assembled atomic weapon. Performs functional and limited mechanical surveillance of atomic weapons in storage. Inspects Relative Humidity Indicators to insure moisture-proofness. Disassembles, inspects, and adjusts mechanical components of atomic weapons. Performs mechanical assembly and test of atomic weapons to insure readiness for use. Inventories weapons and replaces damaged and depleted parts. Directs painting, stenciling and packaging of atomic weapons and association associated containers.

tarantula had been quicker. I was astonished by the existence of a spider that could prey on a mammal.

The other CQ memory was not benign: discovery of the battalion TO&E, the bound volume lying on a desk. Opening it, I quickly found the sheet describing my "Primary Military Occupational Specialty." Alert, prickly, listening intently for anyone approaching the office, ready to dissemble, I read my own job description. Perhaps the document was not even classified, but maybe it was; heavy stuff all the same. Breathless urgency sparked me – anyone might come along, but this was a wildcard chance to see behind the secrecy of months, my head filled with Major Grieden, the Rosenbergs, this rampaging Joe McCarthy. With the dawning of shaky intent I found thrilling, I got a notebook from my car, and furtively wrote out my PMOS, code 431.10, *Atomic Weapons Mechanical Assembler*. This was hard proof, in terse and sketchy boilerplate, telling me what I was – though not who:

ATOMIC WEAPONS MECHANICAL ASSEMBLER- 431.10
"Assembles, modifies, and performs surveillance of atomic weapons and associated equipment. Installs, tests and adjusts mechanical components using mechanics (sic) common and power tools. Prepares atomic weapons for nuclear arming. Tests electrical length of cables using cable tester. Assists in FAT test (sic: Final Assembly Test) to determine acceptability of assembled atomic weapon. Performs functional and limited mechanical surveillance of atomic weapons in storage. Inspects Relative Humidity Indicator to insure moisture-proofness. Disassembles, inspects and adjusts mechanical components of atomic weapons. Performs mechanical assembly and test of atomic weapons to insure readiness for use. Inventories weapons and replaces damaged and depleted parts. Directs painting, stencilling, and packaging of atomic weapons and associated container."

XXII
Fat into the Fire

Not a bad way to live, eh? This from Logan after our return from Fort Sill, where Sarge had not fired a shot, but had found some good beer...

Yeah, well, it was OK, I guess. The money'll come in handy.

Later, when the match scores arrived, I was pleased to see I had placed 204th in a field of 1400. In three months' practice I had made that well-worn, plain vanilla, M-1911A1 .45 my own, shooting against guys with finely tuned customized weapons shooting precision ammo. Even Moose acknowledged my feat, obliquely, in a sardonic aside to Red,

You cain't mess with him anymore now, he's a expert, don't piss him off...

The question of re-upping was now clearly in the air. I perceived that I was valued. I couldn't have specified why. Negative values are indeed values and just thinking about re-upping made me feel weak inside. Soon I saw that this was going to be a game, like everything in the Army. Thus I began to play it as a silent contest of will. I was now aware of the interest of the brass in my decision. Typically I couldn't focus on a future certainly on its way. I hedged and held my cards close, my inner spectator observing as the cadre began to actually woo me. I felt obliged to be cagey. The system taught you to be adversarial; it lay ever in wait for the unwary, like that big tarantula under the barrel cactus. I would say,

I'm thinking about it...

What you got waiting for ya if ya get out? Logan asked one day. He said "if" not "when."

Well, I been thinking some about college...

Hell, the Army'll send you to college, and pay you too.

Oh yeah?

Yeah – I don' know the details, ask Personnel, but they paid for the Colonel's PhD. And McAllister, too – he got a Master's Degree on Army time.

Hmm...

But I continued to drift, sometimes drinking beer until too late to eat supper at the mess hall. There was an encounter with McAllister, now a "Spec-5," the electronics man of alleged 170 IQ who had held the radar meter during the ORI. One long afternoon-evening session at the beer garden with several others brought loud and tipsy praise for this personable lifer, a true genius not often seen in the crummy joint. The question arose inevitably:

What the hell is a guy as smart as you doin in the fuckin Army? The query was echoed and repeated. Some wouldn't give up on it. McAllister, mild-mannered, quiet and well-liked, was the only man in the 14th who could talk to those stuffed-shirt missile engineers. He had a wry sense of humor and might test a new recruit by sending him to the supply room: "Go requisition a can of green electrons."

You're wasting your life here! How can you stand this shit? somebody said. And so it went, McAllister avoiding the question while we sucked up suds and the sun went down, missing chow and making do with beef jerky or pickled eggs until finally, putting the matter to rest once and for all, the radar man held up his hand for attention, and said, slurring his words and shaking his head sorrowfully,

Do you guys realize, I mean realize! – do you realize, if I left the Army, I actually have to WORK?

One man in the whole battalion clearly had no interest in my re-enlistment quandary: Gene Wicket, Battalion Top Sergeant, an E-9. Short and wiry, affable, a quiet man who only his wife ever saw when he needed a shave, he was an ordinary guy, ever ready to talk hunting. Ducks on the base came up at coffee.

What kind are they? Wicket answered in a way you knew he knew:

Greenwing teal, early migrators, excellent table fare. Shortly, our conversation expanding, Wicket offered to lend me a shotgun to try and bag some of the little dabblers before they flew on to Mexico.

Well, I said, *Vessey's a good man, but I don't think he'd cook a duck just for me.* Vessey was our lavishly open-handed Mess Sergeant.

That's all right – you git a duck and me'n Becky'll take care of you.

Wow! This guy was great!

Wicket continued,

You don' have to worry bout a huntin' license if you stay on post, but you do have to get out early in the mornin' an' get back for work. When I went for the gun, he gave me an old topo map of White Sands with the water tanks located on it. Passing our work compound on a morning hunt very early, I saw a five-ton semi leaving it, understood that it was hauling away warheads we had worked on the day before, headed for who knew where.

"Water tank" is a misleading name for these excavated ponds with low earthen walls around them. I quickly discovered I had to park well away from them, go down on all threes and avoid cactus and other thorny stuff, and most important, move quietly to get close enough for a shot when the birds jumped off the water. It took me a week, going out before reveille, to get a first shot. The teal were speedy. I missed every one. Shotguns were a different breed of firearm. But one morning a mallard jumped off the water straight up. My shot connected and the duck fell with a splash in the middle of the pond. Now what to do? Too cold to swim. No wind. The bird might float beyond reach for hours, and the work clock was ticking. Some hundreds of yards away in the car was my fishing rod and tackle box. I ran for it and got a multi-hooked bass plug, and after many casts finally snagged the carcass and reeled it in. Suddenly there was Wicket, smiling at my tactic, having approached unnoticed.

What're you gonna do now? he said.

Gut it, I suppose... My knife was already in my hand.

You don' need a knife for that.

Whaddya mean?

First Sergeant Wicket broke off a prickly mesquite twig and cut off all the thorns but one, near the thick end.

See how the prickers curve back? He inserted the trimmed twig, thorn end first, into the bird's cloaca, twisted it slightly, extracted it – out came the twig with an impaled loop of gut, which he proceeded to extract by hand until no more was left to pull; he broke off the intestine and handed the duck back to an amazed onlooker, saying,

That's all you need to do to field dress a duck; works every time.

It can fairly be said that romantic warmth washed through my alienated heart at that instant and grew, swelling with fantasies that were as much filial as fraternal, but my outward behavior did not change as I took in Wicket's camaradery, his humor, his unassuming solidity. In short, I had found a man who held out simple human acceptance of me in a way no one had ever done. The supper, for which he supplied a second duck, one bird being insufficient for the three of us, was a candlelight affair of good feeling and great cooking – but no alcohol, despite which I was euphoric for days. We talked until late in the evening, his wife keeping a genteel smiling silence before departing upstairs. She thanked me when I thanked her for cooking up this feast. Master Sergeant Gene Wicket never said a word about re-upping and acted as if he couldn't care less about the Army himself, though he was obviously a guy you wouldn't dream of asking for anything that smacked of favoritism. His low-key way and open leathery face, twinkling blue eyes, let this novice shotgunner feel free to tell stories, including my run-in with Moose back in the early days, complete with the foul swine reference in his drunken threat. Wicket interrupted me,

Well, he's from Kansas, ain't he? So he knew what he was talking about, eh? He said no more about the reference to bestiality but continued,

Moose grew up poor, don't be too hard on him for that, he's not a bad man.

But he said he'd kill me.

Talk's cheap – beside, you said he was drunk. I wouldn't worry. Army's the right place for people like him.

Wicket had seen combat in the south Pacific, WWII, island-hopping he called it, had earned a Combat Infantry Badge. I let that sink in and then, fighting sudden shyness, I jumped in and asked if he'd had "to kill anybody out there." He nodded, face suddenly ironlike, his gaze riveting me.

Yeah. Once. He paused long enough that it seemed he had said all he intended; then he continued,

We were inland, had taken the island, only moppin' up left. A sniper was taking our guys, two three a week, killed a couple of men. We knew where he was – certain grove of palm trees – but we couldn' see im – he never fired at night or dim light, could never see a muzzle flash. I just got fed up one day, havin' to sneak around, couldn' stand upright, so I just started crawlin' out there, real slow, ground all tore up by artillery, hotter'n hell of course, I didn' know where I was going or where I was most of the time, knowin' he might git me any time.

Not once did he say "Jap" – you almost never heard any other term.

Were you scared?

Hell yes – dumb question! Be a fool not to be scared! Anyway I began to give up, couldn' see anything, sweatin' like a hog, face in the dirt, didn' wanna go back without... Didn' know what to do. So after awhile I just rolled over on my back, real slow, and I'll be damned, I was looking straight up at him, and he didn' know I was anywhere around, poor guy. All I had was a pistol, .38, never went anywhere without it.

You shot him?

Yeah. Once. They tied themselves into the tree with this long sash. He didn' fall, not even his rifle. Had to leave him up there. His voice was low and dryly mournful by the end of the tale, and in the candlelight I swear I saw wetness around his eyes. It was not in my mind to ask, *How'd you feel afterward?* but he shook his head slightly, as if the question was in the air:

Had to do it – no other way.

And then, the mood lightening, we talked more hunting, satisfying for me to listen to. I'd never found this kind of genuineness at the beer garden; this camaradery watered my desiccation. Even so I still held a kind of reserve, reflexively denying my good feelings, habitual morbid suspicion: "*This is too good to last.*" The evening ended.

Even Supply Sergeant Kayo got to buttering me up for re-enlistment, as far back as when I offered to clean the .45 I returned after practice:

Naw – thass my job – you jus' keep on shootin.' I hear you doin' good, man.

That "everybody" was after me to re-up was my perception; truth no doubt lay elsewhere. I was still going to the beer hall after work, bullshitting with the guys until they went to chow, inventing reasons not to go with them. Eventually I warped into a groove with the tall Schlitz cans. I kept busboys from carrying away the "dead soldiers," without saying or knowing why I wanted them. Sometimes I stayed till dusk and walked as if on rails the mile back to barracks, to tumble into bed, done wrestling with demons for the day. Passivity of will blossomed when I was alone. It smothered my action-oriented restlessness. Paralysis in the face of clear choices became a regular annoyance. Branch and Manning were a constant presence night and day. Concentrating on "them and their fate" let me evade dismal shame at my gutlessness. This atheist that everybody thought was so smart was all too aware he knew more words than meanings. Relationships were but external phenomena, not ongoing connections that could be forged and needed maintaining. Inability to deal with myself in moral terms was making me act like any other Christian: a sinner. I wasn't dead from the neck up, just acted like it. Momentary lucidity revealed this useless relic of religiosity and I seethed with the fury of total denial: I was no sinner, there was no moral tinge to this pain.

After awhile I saw why I liked Wicket with such feeling. The genial Arizonan was the same age as my Dad, on whom I visited spells of silent scorn. I had not the words to understand what was in fact compensatory psychic searching. "Mentor" was not in my vocabulary. Our relations were limited, truncated by rank, Spec-4 and Top Sergeant. But Wicket, even if a killer, seemed to know instinctively how to take the sting out of my silent pain and make me laugh. He actually seemed to like me for who I was more than anyone I had known my whole life, more even than Ed Steele. And it made me feel good to see how Wicket cared for the battalion as if they were his people. Who cared that he acted almost like a father to us? And besides he wasn't a father, he talked to you as if he wore the same stripes you did. This was a Top Sergeant, no question about that, but a man you could trust when too many damned non-coms would screw you just for excitement.

I talked with Red about Wicket, about how he approached disciplinary stuff. With his wry grin, Red said,

Yeah – he's the kind of guy who don't chew your ass, just chews out around it and lets it drop out.

At work, during slack times in the depot, we played volleyball in the glaring heat of the tarmac beside our building, a large concrete cube halfway to the launch pads. Moose stripped to his waist for one game and we saw he was covered all over with thin white scars an inch long, startling against his dark tan. Back indoors, he divulged the story after a question I had thought of but did not ask. He had been "on a little toot" in Juárez and got drunk, got a woman. She asked him to buy her a beer afterward. He agreed and she went away to get it. Dressing, his pants back on, he looked to see why she was taking so long, and saw her squatted on her heels in what passed for a bathroom. She was using the shaken beer to douche herself. The sight angered Moose:

Wastin' good beer like that! He hit her and she screamed. Instantly men appeared from everywhere and piled onto Moose, beat him mercilessly and finished by slashing him all over his body with small knives, cutting even the soles of his feet. They then threw him into the street in his skivvies. He somehow found his bleeding way back to the border bridge, where MPs arrested him and took him to the Ft. Bliss hospital.

It happened during a chronic water shortage in the impoverished city.

The tale deepened my growing negativity, made me glad I had stayed away from Juárez. Actually I had gone there once with Red in the old Hudson, early one Saturday. We walked around the tourist shops and Red bought silver jewelry *for gifts when I go home*. We went to a restaurant with a mariachi band and drank only beer – obeisance to *Montezuma's Revenge* – and ate steaks. We gave brief consideration to hanging around for "night life." Red was uninterested in getting a woman, so we went back up the desert 90 miles to White Sands, the Hudson laboring and drinking plenty of oil in the afternoon heat.

Red re-enlisted. His bonus was two grand, he said, not saying for how long he had signed up. He immediately bought a brand new four-door Ford sedan. I was shocked and felt immediately estranged from him. Red, a draftee, re-upping? I felt not the slightest envy of his bonus and new car.

C'mon, let's go for ride. We toured the post. I was indifferent to his voluble enthusiasm and could not respond in kind to his chatter about the smooth quiet ride, the jackrabbit acceleration of the new V8.
Wanna stop for a beer?
OK.
After a couple, Red said,
You know, you'd get a bonus too, bigger'n mine – you're already Regular Army.
Hmm. I said.

Was that the moment I tipped? I took his reaching out dismissively: we were only buddies, two guys similarly situated who at least liked each other. But I continued to stew in my juices silently, just did my job, holding the issue at bay. There was plenty of time. In the work bays it was a time of increased numbers of warheads, no longer configured as bombs. They showed up overnight in the compound, to be worked on and resealed to disappear overnight; it was boring repetitive depot work. Weeks passed. A new filip was added to the protocol: after the caisson was closed and sealed, it became my task to tape its seams to prevent air passage. The tape was thick lead foil, self-adhesive, pounded into close contact with a rubber mallet to make an hermetic seal. *These warheads are bound for a humid climate,* I thought. The final ritual to render these beasts impervious to humidity suited my obsessive streak. The volunteer mentality is often sustained by idiosyncratic, even perverse, passion, self-generated, a form of "holy martyrdom." I pounded the lead tape methodically but would have repudiated anything like "soldierly dedication." But I had volunteered, had to carry through till my tour of duty was up. Months to go. But cynicism regularly leaked out of my mouth in beer hall chitchat and made a new guy say incredulously

RA? You're Regular Army?

Yeah – I'm an original screw-up. How long I kept the battalion guessing my intentions, and how strong the pressure to declare one way or other, and from whom it came exactly is gone; all the psychic churning and pulsing went on behind boring cut-and-dried nuclear handmaid routine, my inner wrangling a formless flux, no dreamtime. Talk of more pistol matches went away. I had not qualified for higher competition with my Fort Sill score. I continued to practice with my own pistol and knew I would eventually "get good" when not constrained by the cost of ammo and time to practice. Good marksmanship, like playing the violin, required extended effort, and my preoccupation was obsessive distraction, procrastination in a pure form.

XXIII
Airdrop

External relief my from torment came in a call for volunteers, for some kind of test drop of equipment by parachute. On the aircraft I was not assigned a specific task. I wondered why I was even there – probably another initiative from those who wanted me to re-up. The plane was a fat-bodied Fairchild down from Kirtland in Albuquerque, like the one from which I'd seen that poor bastard Roman candle down behind the trees at Camp Campbell.

See us there at Holloman, climbing – no parachutes – into the plane's cavernous cargo belly. Its rear door section was removed to make a huge opening to accept a sledlike pallet on which a big load was rigged and tied down with nylon cords gathered into a handful. Chavez, who had rigged the load, held the lines. At the proper moment he would yank them, setting off explosive cutters which would free the load to slide rearward on a floor of closely-spaced ball-bearinged wheels. This was exciting; flying was always a thrill for me, the feeling, the physical sensations – a chance to rise above the heat-mantle of the desert. In due course we took off into the sun-blast, seat-belted in benches along the side walls of the fuselage, perhaps six men counting Logan, who sat opposite with some airmen, hidden by the load and out of sight. The chill of altitude was delicious. We flew uprange for a while, the huge rear opening framing the mysterious and somnolent landscape, the metallic fangs of the San

Andres Range erupting jaggedly through the brownish furze of desert scrub.

We flew an orientation run over the drop zone. Then Chavez positioned himself at the rear corner opposite me, lanyards gathered in his brown hands. The moment came and he yanked the cords. Came a crackling of firecracker bangs, but the load did not move. Swearing, the motor sergeant saw that a cutter up front had failed to fire. He sprang to it and cut the rigging with a belt knife suddenly produced. The load shuddered slightly and began to slide rearward. Seized by the rising drama of the moment, I unclasped my seat belt, a "neat idea" jangling my brain. The plane nosed up a few degrees to let gravity extract the heavy sled; it rolled out the rear. As it cleared the plane this now-standing thrill-seeker suddenly found myself on my butt on the bumpy rollers, arms flailing as the liberated plane lofted, hard. At once I felt pulled toward the opening. I might have followed the load out the door, but flopped onto my belly, frantic fingers somehow managing to evade the frictionless little wheels to find something solid to hook onto.

Then everybody was shouting and cursing as I struggled. Perhaps hands were laid on to help me regain my seat. I buckled myself in, breathing hard, Logan scowling fiercely at me across the now-empty bay. Chavez had a wickedly sardonic but not hostile grin, and when I looked up the pilot was standing in front of me, an Air Force captain screaming above the engine roar and wind rush about this intolerable violation of SOP, this outrageous threat to his perfect Flight Command Record, about the sheer stupidity of this, the trouble for everybody concerned had I gone out with the cargo, the mountains of paperwork he and every man aboard would have to fill out afterward, to say nothing about the time and expense of a recovery mission:

They might not even find you down there – and if they're smart they wouldn't even look! He continued to chew me out, who had by now grasped that I had risked my life to see if the fuckin chutes had opened. How was I to know the plane would bob up like that?

Je-sus Christ! – and what the hell could you have done if they hadn't opened?

My response if any is gone, but it was completely humble, not at all flippant. I clearly heard the captain's final vow: *Well, you can be God-damned sure you'll never crew on a plane I'm in charge of, ever again.*

I was first off the Fairchild back at Holloman and headed directly to our six-by for the trip back to White Sands. Acutely chagrinned, I nevertheless understood on two bases that I faced no formal disciplinary action. One, I saw in the fury of the pilot's tongue-lashing a certain self-referential excess: it was an insult to him personally. Secondly, there were the cases of beer stacked forward against the flight cabin bulkhead: cheap refrigeration that higher brass wouldn't tolerate if they could see it, intended for some Air Force party that evening, which would have been ruined had I not "luckily" stayed aboard. Sarge grumbled at me for making us look bad. I apologized to him, fully aware I had spoiled a good thing, at least as far as it concerned myself. This was to have been a "fun" detail, a welcome break in pallid routine. But I didn't doubt the pilot's angry words, and more missions were coming up. Vividly life-threatening as the incident was, I didn't dwell on it for long. I acknowledged the stupidity of my act – but I had to; where the hell could I have hidden?

The true shock of the incident came later when I learned what the mysterious load was, rigged as an ordinary water mule, a field water trailer like the one on the convoy to Barksdale last summer. But the sled we had dropped carried extra stuff as well. We were to "evaluate" the load for damage after retrieval, in our bay. I went on quick alert when Sarge made reference to getting the warhead out of it.

Warhead?

Yeah – there's a warhead in there.

We had air-dropped a live Mark 6 into the desert!

No – of course it's not armed – you think they're nuts?

But yes, it was complete, the other components in their own containers, cone assembly, detonators, everything lashed down securely by Chavez or the engineers to prevent drop damage, *they hoped*. Detonation was not a possibility, Logan said. This new HE was perfectly stable. They lied, successfully. At a certain point I thought I should quit asking questions, fearing answers I didn't really want to hear but, but involuntarily prickled by a morbid interest, I found myself asking,

What's it rigged this way for – why would anybody put a warhead in a water trailer? I don' understand. Logan, old soldier, was still gruff in the aftermath of my tumble and would not bite. That pissed me off: did he think he could get me to re-up by treating me this way? My curiosity went unaddressed until quitting time, when I encountered Gene Wicket in the office, who said genially,

How'd it go?

OK – well, I screwed up. You didn't bullshit this guy, or even want to. I told him the story, sketchily; possibly I blushed. Wicket merely grinned his small crooked grin, as if my near-miss was totally predictable but would certainly not upset his digestion.

You are sumthin' else, he said.

The pilot really chewed my ass.

I'll bet he did. He did not follow with 'I sure would have' – but he might have thought it; that's what made this top kick so great.

Then, off-handedly as I could, probably not fooling the old pro at all, I queried the Top Sergeant of the 14th Ordnance Battalion about the purpose of this mission. Silent for a moment, he shrugged and said blandly,

Dunno really – maybe a booby trap...

A booby trap? For what?

Dunno – a city, maybe...

We looked at each other, my mind racing, gooseflesh starting. Conjecture? Reality? I would not have admitted to horror at the ghoulish implication of his words. A shocked response was in my mouth but it wouldn't come out. Every soldier learns it automatically: *Go along to get along.* Wavering, a thousand flashing thoughts ended at potential ramifications should I push this inquiry further. Paranoia? Master Sergeant Wicket might just respond with career-Army bullshit about how a nuclear booby trap, in some future we could never know, might be a military necessity "for a greater good." From my hungry perspective, this man had seemed from the beginning absolutely trustworthy, the first guy I had met who might even become a friend, not just a top kick. But now it dawned on me that I actually knew very little about Gene Wicket or what he stood for really, all of this twinkling by at light speed as I stood there, the moment elongating. I hadn't the courage to press on, not because of possible career-soldier boilerplate from him, nor intimidated by the security angle either. I was ignorant of possible contexts, of potential nuclear scenarios, to ask the "right" questions. I turned away from what I feared might boggle my mind and expose my naïvety.

Also in my mind was that I did not want to learn from his own mouth that Wicket was just another suck-egg lifer. Possibly I grunted as I turned to leave, but he asked gently,
You alright?
I said,
Yeah, Sarge – goodnight.

In this grand matrix of dreamtime stuff, grounded truths, data, are indeed afloat in this noisome stew, some pieces as significant as slippery. Teasing out cause and effect becomes virtually impossible, no hard truths but rather alternatives explicable by many different perspectives. What is sure is that I was stunned by Wicket's remark, his surmise about the purpose, if surmise it was. Profound revulsion stirred my gut at malignant implications of the project, my mind going to an impossible brink, which I had to swallow. I was no whistle-blower and anyway, to say something would be futile from the start. What would I say, and to whom? The question would be gulped down and disappeared; it could only make me look bad. Maybe there was zero risk of making a pariah of myself. Yet I was sick at my gutless silence over this hideous "knowledge." Later I resorted again to the vague notion of "bearing witness," as I had with Earl's predicament back in Albuquerque. I'd never heard of Arthur Koestler's "duty to know."

A long time later the air-dropped warhead had still not come back to our bay. I realized I could not swear before a judge that it had been in fact a Mark 6. All Logan had said was "warhead, yes a live one."

Oh the engineers got it, he said when I found a casual way to inquire about it; that was all he said. The ambiguity of my ethical dilemma became an itch, challenging my rigid "atheism." Denying God with acrid fervor, still, at times I behaved – wordlessly – as if sooner or later I would have to take on the problem of evil – ethical, philosophical, moral, whatever – *on my own.* I wouldn't admit for years to hunger for a source of ethical value outside religion. Did I know what I was doing? No. Years passed before I could stand beside myself and distinguish corroding moral threads that were mine alone to deal with.

I was still going to the beer hall after work, alone now, guys waving in passing but no longer coming over to sit. Suddenly, irrefutable evidence I could not ignore was there: when I counted the empty Schlitz cans on my table one night there were eight. I had drunk eight pints, a whole gallon of beer at one sitting. I told the crew about it next morning, groggy, bragging in mock sorrow how I had still been able to make the walk back to my bunk. Shortly thereafter I quit going to beer call at quitting time. I didn't throw away the precious Jack Daniels, and made no teetotaller resolution, I just quit going. Beer was getting to me. I needed a clear head. Or perhaps a competing addiction, "self," proved stronger than the beer habit.

I went back to walking the desert, out the barracks door away from people, stiff-backed, now finding little diversion in this forlorn scrub littered with rocketry junk the same as before. Maybe I shot at a jackrabbit or didn't, but the feeling was gone that the desert was watching me. I couldn't tell time by the sun in those days, and had no watch, so I just marked time till I thought the dining hall was open for chow. Something had changed; still I lingered out there, aware of a rudimentary sentiment I couldn't begin to honor, a feeling that the desert held important secrets for me, wild or even mystical ones having nothing to do with nuclear weapons. It did and still does; I know now, but my denial then was too solid to perceive. On one occasion, leaving the barracks rapidly, I swung the metal door to, but a stiff gust kept it from latching and it swung wide open and let a swirl of dust inside. Outraged yells erupted,

S'matter with you, Ellis, YOU BORN IN A BARN?

Yeah! I yelled with savage sarcasm, *and every time I hear a jackass bray I get HOMESICK!*

Hung up, frustrated and unable to grasp, to get into this austere mysterious place, or fathom the fugitive traces of lives I could never know, skittering lizard tracks, random turds, tantalizing holes aerating mounds of thorny mesquite, I sought tangible sign of living things everywhere I walked. I shot a magnificent six-foot black and yellow diamondback rattlesnake. I severed the rattles from the zebra-striped tail, "hard proof," a greenhorn's fetish which had a short life, soon discarded. Furious, feeling I could not know a world I couldn't name, I hungered to understand what I could honor only in stumbling ignorance highlighted by these solitary treks.

I laugh at how long it took – years – to realize that ignorance itself could be, should be honored.

Before my twenty-second birthday came a sexual encounter with a prostitute in Juárez. Zooming across the desert with Red, flying in the new Ford, both of us in a go-to-hell mood, we wound up in a bar suitably convivial, drank beer, and I did it. Promptly – and yes! predictably, fell in love with the woman. Mindless infatuation, an overwhelming hunger for intimacy of whatever sort, long held at bay in the grind of days and months. I suppose it served to dissolve adolescent doubts I would never have admitted to myself. Perhaps too it was a silent yielding to peer insinuation defied for months, from the other guys, especially Moose.

A month later I went back to the border in the old Hudson, looking for "Angelina." I searched the district unsuccessfully, remembering some bars, drinking a beer in each but keeping the ladies at bay, getting tipsy and at last, seeing a place I had never been in, I tried it with waning hope, hearing loud palaver and music within. Stairs descended immediately from the threshold, three or four. Beside the lowest step, on a red sofa, was a painted woman whose makeup did not conceal a hard feral visage and who whirled up snakelike and grabbed my crotch painfully, squeezing threateningly. I had never seen this woman in my life. There was no concrete reason for her hostility, but aggressive she was. Shocked bewilderment. I would have done anything to appease her. Only when I muttered some incoherent, fumbling nonsense did she let go. Completely illiterate in Spanish those days, I nevertheless got her meaning when she said,

¿*Que pasa, gringo?* She laughed raucously on learning my mission, and loudly announced my quest to everyone in the joint, who understood and howled uproarious jeers at me. Stunned by the barbaric encounter, I fled back into the rainy September night, revolted by the venereal squalor of this gutbucket business, my mind a caricature of mixed hurt and powerless macho anger and wounded foolishness. The chill air cut through my beery stupor as I trudged through the night, shoulders hunched against light rain, back to the border bridge. Getting another woman was the furthest thing from my mind – it wouldn't be Angelina in any case. Face to face with my venality, I reviled myself at these foolish feelings, this totally childish fantasy of bonding with a woman whose features had already begun to fade from my memory, though I denied so even as I bitterly faced that this thing would never, *could* never have been "reciprocal" in any way. How stupid I was! Yet grief persisted which only time dissolved. Through dank and sour streets I walked, resisting weeping, nausea coming on, from beer or "heartbreak" I couldn't tell and didn't care, in a black despair more puerile than juvenile.

I never went back to Juárez, turned down every invitation from my barracks mates to "go get our ashes hauled." Now I saw only a squalid fornication industry servicing GIs from across the Rio Grande. I had told Angelina I was "cherry" that night, evoking affectionate tenderness leading to a quick virginal spasm that could not have been further from orgasm but was no less intense for that. It was my first, and the only encounter of its kind for years, and long fueled my fantasies, notwithstanding that everybody said those women vied for first-time guys, presuming them not illogically to be disease-free. Could that – cynically – account for her "tenderness?" Regardless, my feelings persisted. From her I had felt special sympathy unattributable to just money, I thought. The guys said you could even play that game, get it cheaper if you were a good actor. The señoritas of Juárez lowered their price for virgins. And the best time to go, they said, was in the last few days before payday – prices were lower then.

In my mind was the image of Moose's white scars. But his tale of drunken criminality was nothing that could happen to me that night. I was looking to be a lover in my search for lecherous initiation. After the quick session, still impaled on the hook of concupiscence, I clumsily maneuvered through the flimsy curtain of her tiny cubicle into a dark corridor hardly one body wide, wobbly from double causation, my nostrils sucked in a musty smog of beer, sweat, tobacco, cheap perfume and the evanescence of stale spilled oats and urine that clotted my senses.

Upon emerging, I had to pass a nurse's station, several mature women sitting against a wall. I was made to drop my khakis and underwear to let a placid, uniformed *mujer* with capable brown hands gently address my slipperiness with a fresh white towel. Opening a tube of *Salvarsan*, she anointed all around and ended by squeezing the remainder of the white ointment into the urethra. High but watching detachedly at first, I went along with her businesslike clinicity, which made me feel "taken care of," which I tried to resist even as my flesh found her soft ministrations more than agreeable. Thus conflicted, raw nature reasserted itself and began to rise again right there in front of everybody. Several women sitting nearby smiled. I giggled, then made as if to shove it toward the nurse, seated at eye level with it, whereupon she barked like a sergeant and smacked it, not hard, but sufficient to make it, and me, wilt into what I really was, an ordinary dogface soldier in a border town whorehouse, dick wrapped in a toilet paper "bandage," dipping toward the queasy pit of another hangover.

Sudden serendipity on the walk back to the bridge: faint quavering tremolo notes in the wet sky, undulating and distant but coming nearer, wild questing honks that pierced my misery like sweet icicles. I stopped and stared up, let tiny raindrops speckle my face. The birds were close but invisible in the flowing overcast, a clarion chorus rising in waves to a clangorous effulgent glory that prickled my whole body, fading away with the southbound passage of the flock. The low clouds were washed with a cheerless tangerine glow as if Cuidad Juárez were burning. The wild clamor of the geese was a teaching, though I didn't recognize it, absorbed, straining to hear it long after the wild music had dissolved in the gentle hiss of the rain. An unforgettable, transfiguring moment it was, a turning point in my burdened passage – or was it? Can such an abstract thing as "transfiguration" be latent for decades and still be called such?

For weeks I studied my crotch, examined myself obsessively for the dreaded *chancre*, for had I not been smart enough to take those raunchy basic training films to heart?

Is not decision necessarily verbal, articulated in words, without which the Rubicon is not crossed? Or can it be self-silent and subconscious? I had no "Aha!" moment. The decision was a knowledge, suddenly simply there, how long I couldn't tell. Had I dreamt it and then failed to remember on waking? Possibly – I was having night dreams again, though seldom recalling their details. I thought it curious how, searching memory, I could find no shred signifying the negative decision. But I didn't go round telling people immediately that my intention had congealed. "Game mode" had to govern the slow tedium of the remaining days.

Well, what would you study if you went to college? Logan asked at coffee, in his most solicitous uncle voice.

Perhaps "forestry" was already in my thoughts, but my answer was a light self-deprecating reference to my ignorance, as if details were not something I had pondered yet. I was acting normal, lying evasively, trying to be just another GI.

You're not ignorant, you're a real smart feller, said Sarge, *and we'd hate to lose you.* I seemed to be back in good graces with Logan after the air-drop fiasco.

Yeah, echoed Moose, *you're a real fart smeller – OH! I mean smart feller!* His mock embarassment was passive-aggressive, and the hostility stung, though I had not the psycho-jargon to name it. Later he said,

You'd make Spec-5 in no time. Better think about it. I felt an overwhelming urge to escape, to run from these abrasive surroundings, this heat and dust, this inane chatter, get the hell away forever from these used-up time-servers who saw nothing beyond bitching and a cold beer at the end of the day.

Well, we'll see. I said.

October came, and deer season. Late on opening morning I crossed San Agustín Pass and found a road, ungated, which let me into outwash hills above the flat desert expanse of the *Jornado del Muerte*. Coronado's conquistadores, searching for the yellow metal that makes men crazy, had fallen to heat and thirst in great numbers here. It didn't look like deer country to me, but I walked in. Other hunters were there. One had shot a small buck before dawn and was leaving with it slung over his shoulder. I met an old man and his wife, and we greeted each other.

We're too old to hunt – but too young to give it up, the man said.

In a short time, seeking information, me believing they were "natives," a lively conversation sprung up, about the lay of the land, the waterholes, about what I might expect: "Not much." As the morning chill dissipated in warm sunshine, the woman offered me coffee. We exchanged names: Jack was short and paunchy, with watery blue eyes, with an uncut beard under a huge straw cowboy hat. His gnarled hands held a .30-30 that seemed to have followed him all his days. Val was grandmotherly, solid and warmly brown-eyed, her face of weathered serenity. I looked around for a place to sit with the coffee and started to perch myself.

Better look under that rock first, Jack said. The flat rock, when I turned it up, immediately revealed a brownish two-inch scorpion running around in circles pugnaciously flexing its stinger. Shocked, I dropped the rock back in place.

Don' wanna sit there! I said. I looked around; no other stone was available. I solved the problem by squatting on my heels, but failed to see a small round sand-colored cactus, which promptly stung me.

OW! I jumped up and felt my butt, felt a bristly fuzz of spines stuck in my jeans. Propping the rifle so it did not lay on stony ground, I carefully pulled the denim away from my skin, twisted around and tried to pluck the spines, but did not succeed. In a few seconds, my holstered pistol and belt knife removed, I lay across Val's knees, pants and underwear down. After awhile she said she had gotten all the "prickers" she could see, apologizing for her "old eyes." I thanked her effusively, burning with embarassment at this tenderfoot show, but they said it could happen to anyone, maybe even had, and they chuckled over some warm mutual memory while I put myself back together, avoiding brushing the fiery spot on my *gluteus maximus*. I wound up staying with them through the afternoon, talking, getting to know them, eating an egg salad sandwich Val offered, listening to Depression stories, our talk punctuated by occasional distant rifle shots. Once there was an echoing volley that clattered forever among the hills.

Durn El Paso redcoats! More money than good sense! Jack said, going on to tell how *cartridges was precious back then. This here old piece kept us in food in the '30s, jackrabbits mostly – hard times before the uranium come in.*

It turned out, according to Jack, I would have to walk in a couple miles if I really wanted a deer and should start early in the morning. It sounded like a project of totally uncertain outcome. I gave no further thought to hunting here. They invited me to their place in Las Cruces for supper. I accepted, and on the way, stopped to check the Hudson's oil in a clearing, a trash-littered cottonwood grove. They pulled in behind me, and when I had finished adding oil, I offered to show them what I could do with my pistol. Jack eagerly assented, so I stood five beer bottles on a fallen log, turned and walked toward the couple standing by the cars, then spun dramatically, drawing as I came around and smashed the five bottles with six shots from the hip, greatly astonishing myself, for the targets were not at "point-blank" range.

Hoo-boy! said Jack, *I'd sure want you on my side in a jackpot!*

But our incipient friendship was not to be. I visited them three or four times in following weeks, but grew uncomfortable with a certain filial tinge of feeling for them. I was drawn to them in a way I somehow couldn't justify. Without doubt the notion of "surrogate parents," spoken aloud, would have seemed outlandish, "embarassing," maybe even "perversion." Yet I liked them, which conflicted me in a way I couldn't resolve. They had a son at sea in the Navy, who was coming home on leave soon and who – they were sure – would be glad to meet me. The man was a submariner, classiest of the naval élite, big and strong and silent as if permanently fathoms deep. Perhaps, after six years' service, he was. Once this sailor opened his mouth I was battered into silence by authentic and revolting red-white-and-blue *gung ho*. He was genial enough, but after displaying his deep allegiance to the US Navy he really wanted to talk about football. That was enough for me. Invited to join them for Christmas dinner, I lied easily and said I already had an invitation, when in fact I had foresworn forever participating in anything Christian, knowing I could never explain my "atheism." If I tried, it would only hurt them, which they didn't need at their age. And I couldn't imagine how I would spend that much time with the son.

The darkness of winter came with biting westerly winds, making desert walks unattractive. I passed free time in patterned fashion; time dissolved into blank featureless ennui. Often I ended up in the bar in Cruces, drinking Jack Daniels alone. At work, a newly assigned lieutenant encountered me in the bay one afternoon, as I listlessly bonked a caisson with the rubber mallet long after it had been sealed.

What are you doing? the officer said, mildly.

Just bonking, sir.

Why I was by myself is gone, my crewmates gone somewhere. Under the lieutenant's quizzical gaze I stirred myself, went to start the hot roaring machine to dry desiccant; I was millimeters from losing self-control. If anyone had asked me just then about re-upping I'd have said "Hell no!"

A new Exec Officer had joined A Company, an outgoing cheerful First Lieutenant, Russell Davisson, still an unknown quantity to us enlisteds. I was caught off-guard when I met him unexpectedly at the end of a day.

How about joining me and my wife for Christmas?

Uh, no sir, thank you very much.

You going on leave? You going home?

Many were leaving; I was not, but I couldn't lie as I had to Jack and Val,

No sir, I'm not.

Well, then please, come to us. There it was again, the atheism question. I didn't know this man, had no idea what his response would be if I told "the truth." I responded in character, recognizing that his plea, outwardly polite, was cast in imperative mode, probably from long officer habit, but who knew? In the upshot I never said yes, but somehow crossed a threshold into acquiescence amid his cheerful banter. I had never met an officer who chattered. But with months still to go, I didn't take a chance on resisting a superior officer I didn't know.

The event was extremely uncomfortable. The house was full of Christian symbols, crucifixes and a large framed portrait of a golden-haired Jesus, a Bible on an end-table by an armchair, and another book bound in white leather, something about a "pearl of great price." The wife was young, buxom and cheerful and stayed out of sight in the kitchen. Three children of solemn mien set the table, staring at me between trips to the kitchen. When we sat to the feast, Lieutentant Davisson prayed loud and long in a Protestant style and language I had never heard before. I endured it silently. Dinner centered around a big roasted chicken, perhaps a capon, though I wouldn't have known, and as the family began to pick up drumsticks and wings, I kept to my knife and fork, cutting pieces precisely and forking them to my mouth. One of the boys said,

Boy you sure eat chicken funny!

I blushed. Father chastised son. I tried to intervene, saying, *It's OK* only to be reprimanded myself by a host turned suddenly stern:

No! This is family business and you have no part in it. This is an infraction of good manners, which we all recognize but will deal with later. Please pardon us for this breach of etiquette.

Pardon *us*?

I got away from them as soon as I could, but not before learning that First Lieutenant Davisson and all the others big and small were devout Mormons. Years later, struggling against religious bigotry, I realized I had been present at their table as much by theocratic injunction as anything else. Love of one's god was one thing, but Davisson's domestic harshness was anything but "holy," a tyranny I knew well, especially the "wait till later" clause. I had seen all I needed to know about our new Exec Officer.

The Chihuahuan desert seemed to resist being what it was that year. Winter brought endless overcast and damp bone-chilling wind. We had never been issued winter liners for our field jackets, so walking the desert had no appeal. The new year came with a sickle moon in a cold glittering sky and, succumbing to a nostalgia that hardly justified the word, utter rubbish in fact, I drank the last ounce of Jack Daniels, a toast at midnight to the guy I had hunted deer with in the Jemez, wondering if that one was feeling equally foolish doing likewise, as he had insisted we both do this midnight.

What about time zones? I had said. Maybe we argued about it, I couldn't remember.

One evening in February I found myself in the Post Library, a discovery though it had been there all along, housed in a Quonset hut. I was wandering up and down the narrow aisles, no object in mind, just moving, any motion was better than lying on my bunk growing mind-mold while thin slushy snow accumulated on a bleak night that couldn't have been drearier. My eyes came to rest on a paperback edition of *Brave New World*. Ignorant of Huxley, I picked it off the shelf idly, the title seeming to resonate with my condition: waiting for release into a real future. Not expecting much – maybe the book had something to fill up my nothing – I took it back to the barracks. Perhaps it was a holiday weekend, and I fell into it, sucked it up, though just what I sucked up I couldn't say for years, except reinforcement for total hostility to chemicals resembling "soma." And of course this self-seeker, full of fatuous fantasy about impending entry into my own brave new world, this self-centered, rebellious, hungry, thirsty and violent ego identified in some specious way with Huxley's savage. The story's point of view was grimly ominous; all the same it seemed to hold a dark speculative truth that fed my emptiness.

The drear endured all winter, incessant cycles of gray days and black nights. I felt my pulse quicken when Mr. Yardley himself queried me about my intentions:

Headquarters needs to make their plans. You decided yet?

No, not quite. Shortly Sarge added to the pressure: *Don' forget, you need at least a month to clear the post, maybe more. Don' wait till the last minute if that's what you're gonna do...*

I won't.

XIV
The End Game

Exactly when I announced what I'd been sitting on is gone, but spilling the beans changed everything, more dramatically than I could have known. Wicket was gone, retired to his ranch over in Arizona after extending a solid handshake and simple invitation to "Come on up and visit us if you get up that way." But it was not to be. My head was tight with a tunnel-vision of "futurethink" – mixed no doubt with futuredread. I was assigned more and more to duties that kept me away from the work bay. I was put to drying silica gel, or delivering "important documents" – as well as clandestine loafing. I had not really expected make-work, and understood only slowly. I was slipped from the crew so effectively I didn't realize for some time that Red, Moose, Logan and Yardley were back in school, for what I couldn't learn and didn't care. But the dissolution of our camaraderie struck me hard one lunch time. Returning to the bay I still thought of as "ours" after some task elsewhere, I met Red in the hall outside the open door. When he saw me, he suddenly waved to those inside. I got a quick glimpse of a tall gray drape yanked swiftly across the bay, concealing the operations area behind it. That curtain had always been there, had never been used until this moment. My curiosity was piqued about what lay beyond. I didn't realize at first that I was the cause of its deployment until Red apologized clumsily with a sorrowful grin and vague remark about the "Cobra device" inside, seeming to regret his words even as they spilled from his mouth.

What's a cobra device? I asked.
I'm...not supposed to say.
A new weapon?
Yeah.
Nuclear?

He was silent. Trying to deal with dawning estrangement, I persisted:

Thermonuclear?
Yeah; don't ask me anything else, okay?
I couldn't care less; if they don't want me to know, then I sure as hell don't want to know.

I was crazy to feel left out, cut off. It hurt, even though I could hardly wait for the end. This instant severance defined the Army for me in that moment, ratified my decision. Shortly Red himself was gone from White Sands, taking a leave up in Albuquerque to be with his fiancée. They would marry in May and Red wanted me to come to the wedding, timed for just after my termination. I liked Red. He was a good man, but when he re-upped I thought he changed, though likel it was me who had, which however made it easier to decline his invitation.

I worked in the Supply Room the last weeks. Sergeant Kayo was pleasant enough in the circumstances, trying genially at least once a day to persuade me to re-up.

It's never too late, he said.

I steadfastly resisted his entreaties, and one day he said, *I know you a good man, therefore I know you be back, I just know it.*

Ha!

Yeah, I just know it – you like that hunter got caught by ol' bear, got wrapped in his arms, couldn' use his gun, didn' know what to do – so he tickle ol' bear between the legs. Bear let him go pretty soon and he run like hell a long time, and when he look back, ol' bear standin' up on the hill, wavin' at him, Come on back... Army's like ol' bear, you'll be back, I just know it.

Ha!

That may have been the first time Kayo offered me .45 ammo.

Why? I was puzzled.

You a pistol man, you can use it."

I don' even have a .45.

But you a pistol man, you'll have one one day, an' this is free.

No thanks – what would I do with it? I'm going to college, I won't have any time.

It was a standing offer, Kayo said, should I change my mind. It amounted to several thousands rounds, good for practice, standard issue ball ammo in unopened crates, themselves useful objects when empty, he pointed out.

No thanks, Sarge, even if I wanted it, that Hudson'll be so packed I couldn't stuff a silver dollar in it.

But you could use it to trade for stuff.

No thanks.

My time grew short. I was given the long and detailed form listing every office on post from which I had to get signatures from the ranking officer, certifying that I had cleared all pertinent obligations, documentary proof that I had tied up every loose end and owed the Army absolutely nothing more. The final signature would be the Company Commander's after I turned in bunk and footlocker on the day I left for Fort Bliss, my termination station. People left me alone those last few days, seeming listless and uninterested. Only a few greeted me "Good luck, man." Rounding up signatures took forever. Kayo of course had material interest in me right to the last minute. All business, he checked off one by one what Supply wanted back from me. But at the end he turned warmly friendly, leaning on the Supply Room counter, with slight supplication at first, definitely out of character, and finally pleaded outright for my help, saying,

I got to get rid of this .45 ammo, get it off my books, adding that he needed the space for something else. *Take it, man, help me out. Your car's right over there, nobody'll see you.*

My mind was suddenly whirling.

No thanks.

His face hardened. I could not mistake the bitterness in his last words,

You some friend, man. I managed to walk not run out into the bright May sunshine, went and got the CO's signature, the car jammed full and waiting, my spine tingling at the yawning anxiety Kayo's final words had opened.

Of course I could have *"done something"* with .45 ammo. But fear spiked and ruled. Had I accepted his *"gift"* I'd have been stopped at the post gate, or at Fort Bliss, the car searched and *"stolen US goods"* found. Confrontation would follow, with prepared alternatives held out: face Court Martial or even Dishonorable Discharge, for theft of government property. Or else, *"Sign right here"* for a new tour of duty and forgiveness, *"Welcome back Bob, we need you."*

Driving across the burning scrub to El Paso, I was stiff with paranoia that something might still happen. They still had me for 24 hours more, until I had that *DD Form 214* in my two hands. Had I read Kayo right? I'll never know for sure. But I trusted then, and believe now, that only alert creative perception saved me. No proof, no witnesses, nobody but myself and a supply man known for finicky precision in his job. My word against his, this soft-spoken but sharp battalion quartermaster Kayo, who had so slickly disposed of Private Barry a year ago, this genial brown sergeant, a family man who had found snug refuge from Jim Crow and a satisfying life as well, just doing his job according to his lights which were the Army's lights: no holds barred, no offense intended, just doing what had to be done, *"the Army way"* – with a smile. My paranoia, firmly in place, still tortures me, but Kayo had outwitted himself, alerted me when, making his case, he slipped a wispy tell-tale thread into his buddy-buddy invitation: *Nobody'll see you.* Kayo had been after me, no question, it was as real as the greasy steering wheel of this clunky old Hudson I had to coax back east. I missed the irony completely: a trusted and valued acolyte carrying away from White Sands Proving Ground ghastly secrets of coldly-reasoned annihilation I could never tell anyone about, ever – yet unable to trust guys I had worked with side by side for almost three years. I didn't notice then that I was projecting onto them distrust that was entirely mine, except for the business with Kayo.

To be sure, my thought roamed nowhere near the intellectual, emotional and creative leap back to truth of Pleistocene roots: real gratitude for life given us by a beautiful generous planet. Was not this roaring American culture on a rampage, living out a dauntless macho teenage in the 50's, as full of piss and vinegar as any of its immortal youth? For myself, I have to pooh-pooh anyone who says I made such a leap in quitting the Army. It wasn't true. My denial of anything "spiritual" ran very deep. I needed no praise from outside. I was on my own and no one knew, no one could know what it was like. Schizoid bind: I couldn't deal with guilt that seemed bottomless, but sandbagged with deep denial. My assessment of how well I had withstood what the Army inflicted on me was part of that denial, which would continue to grow and become silent phobic hatred of all things military, hooked tightly and silently to nuclear weapons, buttressed by rock-hard certitude held in secret because the world didn't want to hear it. Some things are too implacably, gruesomely dangerous to mess with. Bob Manning had known that intuitively, had valued his ignorance at a high price indeed: enough to risk his life for it. And quite aside from my pathology was rock-bottom political truth, enunciated to me by a suffering Vietnam vet as Americans prepare to bludgeon Iraq: *If you deprive an American of his innocence, he'll kill you.*

When I got to college that fall and started to grapple with goal and purpose, I was also groping unaware and unconsciously toward connections only incidentally related to "knowledge," looking for something, *anything* outside myself that might give authentic relief to a soul-burden that would eventually reach suicidal weight. College science, of course, told me right off what I was all too ready to believe, that I didn't even have a soul…

Wendell, Massachusetts
December 2, 2011

Endnotes

[1] The eye can detect single photons, according to Gary Zukav (*The Dancing Wu Li Masters*).

[2] They lied. In 1956 a plane carrying a nuclear bomb was deliberately crashed at Frenchman Flat in Nevada, to see if it would "go nuclear" on impact alone. It did, and guys were killed by radiation trying to recover instruments at ground zero. Carole Gallagher, *American Ground Zero: The secret nuclear war*; 1993 MIT Press.

[3] The first true case history of radiation poisoning was provided by Louis Slotin. *The Greenpeace Book of the Nuclear Age*.

[4] Ibid.

[5] Heresy originally carried the notion of "ability to choose."

[6] "Shit-on-a-shingle," or Creamed Chipped Beef on Toast (the official name). I liked it and did not share in the general oppobrium that greeted it when it appeared for breakfast.

[7] The M-3 is a cheap, crude .45 caliber machine gun, useful only in hand-to-hand combat, say, "cleaning out buildings."

[8] I had picked up some western lingo by then.

[9] We showed the Mideast how!

[10] Like hell! Nuclear reactors now orbit in deep space...

[11] Carole Gallagher, op. cit.

[12] Troops walked through ground zero immediately after the Priscilla shot in 1957, and came back bleeding from eyes, ears, nose and mouth. Gallagher, op. cit.